# EAT
# WELL
# NOW

*and your body will thank you tomorrow*

# EAT
# WELL
# NOW

*and your body will*
*thank you tomorrow*

## IAN THORPE

hardie grant books

# CONTENTS

# introduction

Many times in my life, I've had to look closely at the way I eat.

As a swimmer, I trained for forty hours a week and focused on stocking up with energy – I literally ate four times more than what I otherwise would have.

In high-performance sport, the truth is you can pretty much eat anything you want to and plenty of it in terms of calorie intake, as you burn all the calories off. To meet my training needs, I needed protein in my diet to help my muscles build and repair, and lots of carbohydrates for energy.

When I stopped swimming competitively, I suddenly found I had a very different lifestyle. I had to dramatically reduce my meal sizes and steer away from the amount of carbohydrates and protein that once filled my plate. In looking back, what I thought of as a standard meal as a swimmer was incredibly warped. But, I didn't want to start going to the other extreme and starve myself either.

My body went through a lot of chemical changes and I had radical cravings for starch! My body cried out for it, and I must admit I gave it what it wanted. I really let myself fall off the track. After years of competing, I let myself relax for once, but after a few months I realised I felt sluggish and tired and I started to see what my diet and lack of exercise was doing to my body. From that point on I decided that I wasn't going to eat like that any more as my body was obviously not responding well to how I was treating it. I wanted to set myself up for how to eat for the rest of my life and I wanted to get it right – which is how these recipes came about. They are a result of looking for a balanced and realistic way to eat well – minus any extremes.

# the way I eat

I am a strong believer that there is no 'good' or 'bad' food, and I don't wish to follow the extreme ups and downs of 'dieting'. I think it's important not to deprive and punish yourself, as it's just not a positive way to live. But I do think we have to limit excessive consumption of the foods that we know don't have a good effect on us – such as sugar, trans and saturated fats, and 'empty' carbohydrates such as white bread and white rice. Also, I think we have to try not to over-eat in general, and become in tune with what our bodies need versus what we might want. It's just about habits really, and once you are on the right track it can become quite automatic.

I believe that the best way to know what you are eating is to cook your food yourself, avoiding processed foods that are high in salt and unbeneficial fats, and lacking in nutrients compared to fresh, natural food. So, as much as anything, I hope this book just encourages people to get into the kitchen and start experimenting with ingredients and flavours, realising as I have that cooking and eating healthily is great fun.

I focus on including a wide range of vegetables, legumes and grains as well as protein in my diet. While I usually start the day with carbohydrates in the form of porridge in winter, or muesli in summer – and I recognise that carbohydrates are absolutely essential – for the rest of the day I try to steer away from carbohydrate-based meals of bread, rice or pasta. In the Western world, I think we eat too much of them, and should be getting more nutrition from vegetables, fruit, legumes and whole grains. When I do eat carbohydrates, I prefer carbohydrates that have higher nutritional benefit and slower energy release – for example, I go for brown rice in favour of refined white rice.

I try to look for alternatives to the common high-carbohydrate accompaniments such as mashed potatoes, couscous and noodles. Instead I cook parsnip mash or white-bean puree; cauliflower 'couscous'; squid 'noodles'; or zucchini 'fettuccine'. I also try to avoid too much sugar and salt in my diet, and when I have fats I aim for them to be monounsaturated or polyunsaturated.

My approach might sound technical – but once you have grasped the few simple ideas behind this style of eating, I believe you can still enjoy what you eat as much as ever, as my food is also about delicious flavours and great combinations, and not scrimping to take any of the enjoyment of eating away.

# how my interest in cooking started

My first memory of cooking is at my nan's house when I was about five or six. This was my introduction to the kitchen. If I was sick from school, I would be at her house helping to make a cake, or smelling the aroma of a cake baking as she made one. Nan is incredible at cakes – but it was the process at work that intrigued me, too. I can always remember being fascinated by how, if you put all these different ingredients into a bowl and then into the oven, they magically transformed into something else.

I started to take an interest in cookbooks and began asking my mum, 'Why haven't we tried this?' I think Mum must have got fed up with me and in the end said 'Make it yourself'. So I did, and began to cook the family meal on a Sunday, which Mum was really happy about because it was a night off for her. Of course there were a couple of disasters, like when I made creamed rice. I remember how drastically I undercooked the rice and it was completely inedible. But that's how you learn. I really had to learn to cook well when I moved out of home and had to take full responsibility for what was going into my meals and my body, to make sure I was meeting my swimming needs. I had to learn a lot about nutrition in order to avoid taking truckloads of multivitamins.

Another thing that led me towards being interested in food was travelling around the world for competitions, and staying in some really nice hotels. The food at these hotels was amazing, but after a couple of weeks you just start to crave simple, home-style cooking, which hotels don't really do. One day I rang someone at the front desk of the hotel where I was staying and asked them if they minded if I cooked something for myself in the kitchen. After it was approved by the hotel's head chef, I went down and prepared myself a meal and I can remember the chef being quite surprised that I cooked. He asked me if I would like to come down and watch the dinner service later on, which I accepted without hesitation.

I ended up spending some time in that kitchen, learning about what went in which dishes, trying this, tasting that. After a few nights, I started to learn some of the recipes that were on the menu. The head chef then asked me if I would like to help cook for the guests, so to everyone's surprise, I started cooking at the restaurant. I remember the first night I cooked an assiette of lamb served on lentils.

I've now cooked at that particular restaurant a couple of times. I've actually taken some friends there and disappeared into the kitchen and prepared half the meal myself. They couldn't believe it!

Some people go away on holiday and want to get massages and that sort of thing, but that's not me. I get bored so easily, so when I go away I like to spend time in different kitchens, learning how to cook in different ways. In Japan I was lucky enough to learn how to cut sashimi properly, plus a few other tricks. I have some fantastic memories of visiting different kitchens around the world. I think one of the great things about food is that it can take you somewhere – back to that holiday you loved, or perhaps to the one you're still dreaming about. And with food, you never stop learning. I've gone from cooking cakes with my nan, to learning about nutrition from an athlete's perspective, to having to readjust to a normal life without the massive exercise regime. And along the way, I've had the good fortune to cook with some great chefs around the world, which is kind of cool.

From all of these experiences has come my passion in nutritious home cooking and sustainable eating for the long term. Healthy food and a healthy lifestyle should be a pleasure, not a punishment. It's all about being aware of what goes into your body and how it affects you in both the short and long term – but still being satisfied by great meals, as delicious food and eating healthily don't need to be mutually exclusive. Eat well now and your body will thank you for it tomorrow.

# BAS
# ICS

# making stocks

Making your own stock from scratch is so easy to do. There's no comparison when it comes to homemade stock versus store-bought. Homemade stock is rich in minerals and contains less sodium and no preservatives – you'll notice a difference in flavour as well. I start to make stock at the first sign of winter when I begin to feel a chill in the air, because I know that I am about to start eating loads of soup. I just love it – I can seriously have it for breakfast.

I often have a 'stock day', a day devoted to making stock, as it's easy to make them all in one go with lots of pots on the stove simmering away. This way, you can get all your stocks made and packed away so they'll be ready to whip out of the freezer when you need them next.

To store stock, I have containers in multiple sizes that are all stackable. I like to store different quantities of stock, from 500 ml to 1 litre. After making stock, I usually transfer about one-third of the cooled stock to the fridge to use within the next week, and then the other two-thirds go into the freezer labelled with the date I made it, and it keeps for about three months.

# CHICKEN STOCK

~~~~~~~~~~~~~~~~~~~~~~~~~~~~~~~~~~~~~~~~~~~~~~~~~~

## makes 3 litres

This is the most important stock I make as I use it so regularly (including in one of my favourite recipes, the Three-day Chicken on page 106). I actually treat my chicken stock like a Chinese 'master stock', meaning that I never use it all up and keep some of the last batch to form the base of the next batch. As a result, my stock has a rich, concentrated flavour – and for some purposes I actually water it down. An easier way of getting a similar flavour is to add a few natural chicken-stock cubes in place of salt, which I have added to this recipe (but if you'd prefer not to use these, then you can just add salt to taste).

3 kg free-range chicken wings
4 celery stalks, roughly chopped
2 carrots, roughly chopped
2 onions, roughly chopped
1 bouquet garni made of 2 bay leaves,
    8 parsley stalks and 4 thyme sprigs tied
    with string
2 natural chicken-stock cubes
3 litres cold water

Use kitchen scissors to cut each chicken wing through the joints to give 3 sections. Put the wings and remaining ingredients in a large pot and bring to the boil. Once boiling, reduce the temperature to a simmer. Use a large spoon to skim the surface of any impurities. Cook gently, uncovered, for 2½–3 hours. Every now and then, top up with a little water to keep it roughly at the original level.

Use a large slotted spoon to remove the chicken and vegetables from the stock, and discard. Pour the stock through a fine strainer into a clean pot. Bring to the boil and skim the surface of any further impurities, then leave to cool. Skim the fat from the surface before dividing into containers and storing in the refrigerator or freezer until needed (frozen stock will keep for up to 3 months).

# RICH BEEF OR
# VEAL STOCK

*makes 2–2.5 litres*

**I add a pig's trotter to my beef stock for extra flavour, along with a generous quantity of tomatoes.**

1 kg beef or veal bones
1 pig's trotter (optional)
1.5 kg ripe tomatoes
2 carrots, roughly chopped
2 celery stalks, roughly chopped
1 onion, roughly chopped
2 garlic cloves

1 bouquet garni made of 4 bay leaves,
    4 parsley stalks and 2 thyme sprigs tied with
    string
6 black peppercorns
2 tablespoons sea salt
3 litres cold water

Preheat the oven to 180°C. Place the bones, pig's trotter (if using) and whole tomatoes in a large baking dish. Bake for 40 minutes, or until the bones are well browned. Tip the contents of the dish into a large pot and add the remaining ingredients. Bring to the boil, then reduce the temperature to a simmer and use a large spoon to skim the surface of any impurities. Simmer uncovered for 4 hours, or until the stock has reduced by half.

Scoop out the bones, trotter and vegetables with a large slotted spoon and discard. Pour the stock through a fine strainer into a clean pot. Bring to the boil and use a large spoon to skim the surface of any further impurities. Strain again and leave to cool. Skim the fat from the surface and divide into containers. Store in the refrigerator or freezer until needed (frozen stock will keep for up to 3 months).

# VEGETABLE STOCK

*makes 2.5–3 litres*

**This stock gets a nice vegetable flavour when it reduces and concentrates.**

16 celery stalks, roughly chopped

12 onions, roughly chopped

8 carrots, roughly chopped

8 parsnips, roughly chopped

1 bouquet garni made of 2 bay leaves,
   8 parsley stalks and 4 thyme sprigs tied
   with string

6 black peppercorns

2 tablespoons sea salt

5 litres cold water

Combine the ingredients in a large pot. Bring to the boil, then reduce the heat to a simmer. Use a large spoon to skim any impurities from the surface. Simmer uncovered for 4 hours, or until the stock has reduced by half.

Strain the stock and discard the solids, and leave to cool. Divide into containers and store in the refrigerator or freezer until needed (frozen stock will keep for up to 3 months).

# making curry pastes

People really notice the difference between store-bought and homemade curry pastes – there are always lots of 'oohs' and 'aahs' at the dinner table. A curry paste made from scratch releases all the subtle flavours and aromas of the fresh ingredients.

When I make a batch of curry paste, I store it in the freezer, measuring out tablespoons into ice-cube trays. After it's frozen, you can transfer the cubes to a sealable bag. Then, it's ready for the next time I need it. Curry paste is not difficult to make and is great to have on hand when you want to cook something easy – as by just adding a little seafood, meat or vegetables and a dash of coconut milk (or my No-fat Coconut Milk on page 20), you have a quick dinner.

And, another great reason to make curry pastes is that they double as flavoursome marinades.

# GREEN CURRY PASTE

*makes 1 cup*

12 long green chillies, roughly chopped
5 kaffir lime leaves, finely shredded
4 shallots, roughly chopped
3 lemongrass stalks (white part only), roughly chopped
2 cm galangal, peeled and roughly chopped
3 coriander roots, cleaned
1 garlic clove, roughly chopped

2 teaspoons shrimp paste
2 cloves
2 teaspoons ground cumin
2 teaspoons ground coriander
1 teaspoon freshly ground black pepper
1 teaspoon sea salt
2 tablespoons vegetable oil

Put the ingredients other than the oil in a food processor and pulse until well combined. Pour in the oil and blend for 4–5 minutes, or until smooth.

Store in an airtight container in the refrigerator for up to 10 days, or freeze in an ice-cube tray and transfer the cubes to a sealable bag.

# RED CURRY PASTE

*makes 1 cup*

15 dried long red chillies
5 kaffir lime leaves, finely shredded
4 shallots, roughly chopped
3 lemongrass stalks (white part only), roughly chopped
6 coriander roots, cleaned
5 garlic cloves, roughly chopped
2 teaspoons shrimp paste

2 teaspoons ground coriander
2 teaspoons ground cumin
2 teaspoons ground cloves
1 teaspoon sea salt
1 teaspoon freshly ground black pepper
2 tablespoons vegetable oil

Put the chillies in a bowl and cover with boiling water. Soak for 30 minutes, until rehydrated, then drain and roughly chop.

Put the chillies and remaining ingredients other than the oil in a food processor and pulse until well combined. Pour in the oil and blend for 4–5 minutes, or until smooth.

Store in an airtight container in the refrigerator for up to 10 days, or freeze in an ice-cube tray and transfer the cubes to a sealable bag.

# HARISSA

*makes half a cup*

I try to prepare something like harissa, nahm jim or a curry paste once a week, so that I always have a range of flavour bases on hand for whipping up quick meals. These sauces and pastes keep a long time, and I think they save me time in the long run and make meals taste great without too much effort.

30 g dried long red chillies
1 tablespoon black peppercorns
1 teaspoon caraway seeds
2 tablespoons dried mint
1 tablespoon ground coriander

1 tablespoon ground cumin
1 teaspoon ground ginger
8 garlic cloves, roughly chopped
1 tablespoon sea salt
80 ml olive oil, plus extra for the jar

Put the chillies in a bowl and cover with boiling water. Soak for 30 minutes, until rehydrated, then drain.

Combine the peppercorns and caraway seeds in a mortar and grind to a powder. Transfer to a food processor along with the chillies, mint, ground spices, garlic and salt and pulse until just combined. Slowly pour in the oil and continue to blend for 3-4 minutes, or until smooth.

Transfer to a sterilised jar and cover with a thin layer of oil. Store in the refrigerator for up to 6 months.

# NO-FAT COCONUT MILK

*Makes 500ml*

This is a fantastic alternative to coconut milk. Although I love regular coconut milk with its rich, creamy taste, if I am having more than one curry a week I'll quickly whip this up. It is the best alternative I have found as it cooks in a similar way to coconut milk, but it won't have you feeling guilty.

1 cup skim-milk powder
500 ml water
1 tablespoon coconut essence

Whisk all the ingredients together in a bowl until combined.

# NAHM JIM

makes 1.5 – 2 cups

1 bunch coriander with roots
1 red bird's-eye chilli, finely chopped
125 ml soy sauce
juice of 6 limes
2 garlic cloves, crushed
1 tablespoon sugar
3 cm piece of ginger, peeled and grated
3 tablespoons fish sauce

Finely chop the coriander roots and leaves. Mix all the ingredients together in a bowl. Store in the refrigerator for up to 1 week.

# GREMOLATA

makes half a cup

**Scattering gremolata onto a dish really lifts out the flavours, giving everything a fresh zing.**

1 garlic clove
½ cup flat-leaf parsley leaves, finely chopped
2 teaspoons grated lemon zest
2 teaspoons grated orange zest
1 teaspoon grated lime zest

Bring a small saucepan of water to the boil. Add the garlic clove and boil for 2 minutes, then remove it to a bowl of chilled water to cool.

Finely chop the garlic. Put it into a bowl with the parsley and zest and mix well.

I ALWAYS MAKE SURE MY FRIDGE AND PANTRY IS STOCKED WITH THE ESSENTIALS FOR QUICK MEALS THINGS LIKE MY STOCKS, CURRY PASTES, HARISSA AND NAHM JIM. THE OTHER THING IS TO REMEMBER TO BUY YOUR VEGETABLES AND MEAT ON THE WAY HOME, RATHER THAN COMING HOME TO AN EMPTY LARDER.

# TOMATO SAUCE

*makes 500ml*

This home-style tomato sauce is basically just fresh, ripe tomatoes reduced down to a thick ketchup, with a few extra flavours added. It's different to tomato sauce from a supermarket as it doesn't have so much added sweetness.

4 tomatoes, roughly chopped
1 onion, roughly chopped
85 g (⅓ cup) tomato paste
1 garlic clove, crushed
2 tablespoons red-wine vinegar
2 tablespoons lemon juice

1 tablespoon olive oil
1 teaspoon cayenne pepper
pinch of ground cumin
good pinch of sea salt

Put the ingredients in a food processor and blend until smooth.

Transfer to a saucepan and simmer over low heat for 25–30 minutes, or until the mixture has reduced by half. Pass through a strainer. Store in an airtight container in the refrigerator for up to 2 weeks.

# SUSHI RICE

*makes 4 cups*

2 cups sushi rice
500 ml water
3 tablespoons rice vinegar
2 tablespoons caster sugar
1 tablespoon sea salt

Put the rice in a sieve and rinse under running water until the water is almost clear. Transfer to a medium saucepan, add the water and bring to the boil without a lid. Reduce the heat to low and cook until all the water is absorbed and the rice is tender (about 8–10 minutes).

Meanwhile, combine the vinegar, sugar and salt in a small bowl and stir to partly dissolve the sugar.

Spread the cooked rice out in a flat dish and sprinkle over the vinegar mixture. Stir gently with a wooden spoon until the rice is evenly coated, then cover with a tea towel and leave to steam for 7–8 minutes. Remove the towel and fan the rice for about 5 minutes, until cool.

Cover the rice with a damp tea towel to stop it drying out while you make your sushi.

Side dishes are really what we should be eating and filling up on as they are usually fresh, healthy, vegetable-based and full of nutrition.

It is true that sides are sometimes the opposite of this – take buttery mashed potatoes, a basket of fries or white bread, which are either fattening or offer limited nutrients, or both. But when you change the focus to vegetables other than potatoes, and to beans and lentils and whole grains, then you can fill up on food that actually serves your body well.

Just a note on potatoes – they are high in carbohydrates and have a high GI, but it is not that they don't have anything at all to offer. In fact, they are a good source of vitamin C, potassium, fibre and other nutrients, especially with their skins on. But they often lend themselves to substantial amounts of fat such as cream or butter if they are mashed, or oil if they are deep-fried, and can dominate a meal when other vegetables should be allowed to shine!

When I'm cooking, I always ask myself how can I get more vegetables onto my plate, and side dishes such as the recipes in this chapter are usually my answer. Vegetables are packed full of minerals, vitamins and antioxidants – things that are essential to the functioning of our bodies, and which fight off infection and disease. They are the key to a healthy life.

My favourite side dish of all is the Vegetable Stir-fry with Miso. It's easy to prepare, delicious, and gives you no excuse for eating badly. If I haven't planned my week well and have run out of time to cook food in advance, this is something I can quickly buy the ingredients for on the way home and whip up in a minute. I actually eat it regularly as a light dinner, and might add some tofu or chicken if I have some on hand.

All of these side dishes are easy to prepare and most of them would serve as a perfect light lunch. Or you can serve a few of them for dinner without any 'main' as such – why not?!

SID
ES

# VEGETABLE STIR-FRY
# WITH MISO

serves 2

This stir-fry is really versatile and I cook it often. It can be served alongside grilled meat or seafood or any other Asian-inspired dish. It also works as a quick light lunch if you add some tofu or a little chicken.

1 tablespoon peanut oil
1 bunch choy sum, cut into 3 cm lengths
1 onion, cut into wedges
1 red capsicum, finely sliced
1 carrot, cut into matchsticks
4 cm piece of ginger, peeled and grated
1 garlic clove, crushed
2 tablespoons white miso paste
1 tablespoon soy sauce

Heat the oil in a wok over high heat. Add the choy sum stalks, onion, capsicum, carrot and ginger and stir-fry for 2–3 minutes. Add the choy sum leaves, garlic, miso paste and soy sauce and stir-fry for a further 2–3 minutes, or until the vegetables are tender. Serve straight away.

I DON'T HAVE A LOT OF RICE IN MY DIET BECAUSE – LIKE BREAD, PASTA AND POTATOES – IT HAS A HIGH GI AND NOT A GREAT DEAL OF NUTRIENTS, SO IT IS NOT THE IDEAL FOOD TO FILL UP ON. IF I COOK A STIR-FRY, I'M GENERALLY SATISFIED WITH JUST THE STIR-FRY – AND PERHAPS HAVE SOME PROTEIN SUCH AS MEAT OR TOFU ON THE SIDE. I DO COOK RICE, SUCH AS JASMINE OR BASMATI RICE, IF I'M HAVING PEOPLE OVER FOR DINNER AND COOKING ASIAN, BUT IF IT'S JUST ME – THERE'S NOT A CHANCE. IF YOU DO EAT RICE WITH A STIR-FRY, MAKE SURE THAT THE RICE IS THE SMALLEST PORTION IN YOUR BOWL – AND IF YOU CAN, EAT BROWN RICE, WHICH HAS FAR MORE FIBRE, AND VITAMINS AND MINERALS.

# ZUCCHINI NAPOLETANA SALAD

*serves 6*

In this dish the zucchini is peeled into ribbons and replaces what would usually be pasta such as fettuccine. So, the dish is full of raw goodness. The zucchini is mixed with Tomato Sauce (page 23), and if you can have that made in advance, then the salad is super quick to make and is a great side dish for summer.

10 small-medium zucchini,
    peeled into fine ribbons with a vegetable peeler
500 ml Tomato Sauce (page 23)
4 tomatoes, chopped
¼ cup brazil nuts, finely chopped
12 basil leaves, torn
sea salt
freshly ground black pepper

Combine the zucchini, tomato sauce, tomatoes, brazil nuts and basil in a bowl.
Season with salt and pepper and serve.

THE COLOURS OF FRUITS AND VEGETABLES
ARE KEYS TO THE NUTRIENTS THEY HAVE INSIDE,
SO EATING FROM ALL THE COLOUR GROUPS
ENSURES YOU ARE GETTING A GOOD RANGE,
PARTICULARLY WHEN IT COMES TO ANTIOXIDANTS.
FRUIT AND VEGETABLES IN THE RED GROUP
INCLUDE TOMATOES, STRAWBERRIES AND
WATERMELON; THE ORANGE AND YELLOW GROUP
INCLUDES CARROTS, PUMPKIN AND APRICOTS;
THE GREEN GROUP INCLUDES SPINACH,
CUCUMBER AND KIWI FRUIT; THE BLUE AND
PURPLE GROUP INCLUDES EGGPLANT AND
BLUEBERRIES; AND THE WHITE GROUP INCLUDES
CAULIFLOWER, ONIONS AND GARLIC.

# PARSNIP MASH

*serves 8*

Parsnip mash allows you to enjoy the comfort food that is mash, with fewer carbohydrates than you would find with potatoes and more fibre. Parsnips are also high in potassium and vitamin C. Their earthy, sweet flavour is a welcome change in mash and works well with many dishes.

10 parsnips, peeled and roughly chopped
1 litre Chicken Stock (page 15)
pinch of ground white pepper
1 tablespoon cream

Place the parsnips, stock and pepper in a saucepan and bring to the boil. Reduce the heat to a simmer and cook for 30–45 minutes, until the parsnips are tender and there is only a little stock remaining. Add the cream and use a potato masher to mash the parsnips until smooth, then serve straight away.

# WHITE-BEAN PUREE

*serves 4*

Beans are a great source of protein and fibre, and the carbohydrate they contain is low in GI. So, this puree allows you to fill yourself up on a more nutritious alternative to potato mash.

1 cup dried cannellini beans, rinsed
750 ml water
750 ml chicken, beef or
    vegetable stock
1 garlic clove, crushed

2 tablespoons fresh lemon juice
2 tablespoons olive oil
sea salt
freshly ground black pepper

Soak the cannellini beans in the water overnight or for at least 2 hours. Drain and place the beans in a large saucepan. Add the stock, then slowly bring the beans to the boil. As soon as it starts to boil, reduce the heat and simmer slowly. Check the beans as they cook to make sure they have enough stock to cover. Add water if necessary. The beans should be cooked in 1–2 hours. When cooked, place the beans, garlic, juice and olive oil in a food processor and pulse until smooth. Season with salt and pepper to serve.

# LENTILS DU PUY

serves 4

This dish just rocks. It's a really tasty, earthy accompaniment to chicken or fish.

1 cup small green Puy lentils
2 tablespoons olive oil
2 garlic cloves, crushed
1 onion, finely chopped
¼ cup chopped flat-leaf parsley
750 ml water
sea salt
freshly ground black pepper

Rinse and drain the lentils. Heat the olive oil in a saucepan, add the garlic and onion and cook until soft. Add the lentils, parsley and water, bring to the boil then turn down the heat and simmer for about 20 minutes, or until the lentils are tender but still hold their shape. Season with salt and pepper and serve.

LENTILS ARE ONE OF THE HIGHEST FIBRE FOODS, AS WELL AS BEING HIGH IN PROTEIN AND PACKED WITH VITAMINS AND MINERALS SUCH AS FOLATE, IRON AND MANGANESE. DUE TO THEIR SOLUBLE FIBRE CONTENT, LENTILS CAN HELP LOWER LDL CHOLESTEROL AND KEEP BLOOD SUGAR IN CONTROL.

# GREEN-ENVY VEGETABLES

*serves 6*

This is like a green ratatouille, and is incredibly easy to make – you just throw it all in the oven to bake. It goes fantastically with grilled fish or chicken, which you can cook while the vegetables are in the oven.

6 zucchini, chopped
1 parsnip, peeled and chopped
½ bunch celery, trimmed and sliced
   1 cm thick
1 leek, sliced
1 large yellow capsicum, finely sliced
4 garlic cloves, finely sliced
1 tablespoon chopped sage

1 tablespoon chopped thyme
2 teaspoons olive oil
sea salt
freshly ground black pepper
75 g parmesan, grated
¼ cup flat-leaf parsley leaves, torn

Preheat the oven to 180°C. Combine the vegetables, garlic, sage and thyme on a large baking tray. Drizzle on the oil and season with salt and pepper, then toss lightly.
Cover with foil and bake for 35 minutes, or until the vegetables are tender. Sprinkle with the parmesan and parsley and serve.

I THINK IT'S IMPORTANT TO EAT AS MUCH NATURAL FOOD AS POSSIBLE, AND TO CONNECT WITH WHERE YOUR FOOD COMES FROM WHENEVER YOU CAN. GENERALLY SPEAKING – BECAUSE OF THE WAY WE SHOP IN SUPERMARKETS – MOST PEOPLE HAVE BECOME DISCONNECTED FROM HOW THINGS ARE GROWN, HARVESTED AND MADE. BUT IF YOU WATCHED HOW SOME FOODS WERE PUT TOGETHER FROM SYNTHETIC FLAVOURS AND EXUDED FROM MACHINES, YOU WOULD NEVER EAT THEM!

# a return to the past

I think it's great that people today are venturing back into the kitchen and preparing their own meals, as this is the only way we can know exactly what goes into the food we eat. Preparing food with your family can also be a focal point in your home, and a way that families can explore and engage with each other. It's how I started taking an interest in food and cooking, with my mum and nan.

# QUINOA WITH SILVERBEET

*serves 6*

Quinoa is a great alternative to rice, couscous and other grains (it is actually a seed, but it cooks like a grain).

1 tablespoon olive oil
1 leek, chopped
2 onions, finely chopped
3 garlic cloves, crushed
2 cups quinoa, rinsed
1 litre Vegetable Stock (page 16)
1 lemon, zested, and juiced to give
    1 tablespoon juice

4 sage leaves
1 bunch silverbeet, stems cut into 1 cm slices,
    leaves cut into 5 cm lengths
¼ cup brazil nuts, chopped
2 tablespoons flat-leaf parsley leaves

Heat the oil in a heavy-based saucepan over medium heat. Add the leek and onion and fry for 2–3 minutes, until starting to soften. Add the garlic and fry for another 2 minutes. Add the quinoa and stir to coat in the oil. Add the stock, lemon zest and juice and sage leaves, then cover with the lid and bring to the boil. Reduce the heat to a simmer and cook for 20 minutes. Remove the lid and stir in the silverbeet stems and leaves and the brazil nuts, then cook for a further 5 minutes – the silverbeet stems should still be a little crunchy. Serve garnished with the parsley.

SILVERBEET IS A GREAT SOURCE OF FOLATE, IRON, FIBRE AND VITAMINS A AND C. WHEN SHOPPING FOR IT, CHOOSE BUNCHES WITH UNBLEMISHED, CRISP LEAVES, AND STALKS THAT ARE STIFF, AS THIS MEANS THEY ARE FRESH. WHEN YOU GET HOME, REMOVE THE STRING OR ELASTIC BAND THAT HOLDS THE STEMS TOGETHER AND STORE THE SILVERBEET IN THE CRISPER OF YOUR FRIDGE IN A PLASTIC BAG.

# BRAISED CELERY HEARTS
# WITH BACON

serves 8

Celery is not often served as a feature, but why not? It is delicious and I find this is a great dish for people who claim they don't like vegetables, because the bacon, onion, lemon zest and herbs add a wonderful depth of flavour. It is fantastic served with lamb or beef.

2 bunches celery
½ tablespoon butter
1 tablespoon olive oil
3 bacon rashers, fat trimmed, finely chopped
3 carrots, chopped
2 onions, chopped
4 thyme sprigs

250 ml Rich Beef or Veal Stock (page 16)
4 sage leaves
1 teaspoon grated lemon zest
1 cardamom pod, cracked
sea salt
freshly ground black pepper
¼ cup chopped flat-leaf parsley

Remove any old outer stalks from the bunches of celery, and cut a thin slice from each base if they are brown. Trim the tops to give you 2 celery bulbs of around 15 cm. Set the tops aside for another recipe. Use a vegetable peeler to peel the strings from the outer celery stalks. Cut each bulb in half lengthwise through the base.

Melt the butter in a large heavy-based saucepan over medium heat. Add the celery halves and fry for 2-3 minutes on each side, until starting to colour. Transfer to a plate.

Add the oil to the pan, followed by the bacon, carrot, onion and thyme and fry for 3-5 minutes, or until the bacon is golden. Return the celery halves to the pan along with the stock, sage, lemon zest and cardamom pod. Bring to the boil, then reduce to a simmer and cover with the lid. Cook for 10 minutes.

Turn the celery halves and cook for a further 10 minutes. Season with salt and pepper.

To serve, cut the celery halves in half again, giving quarters. Serve with the bacon and vegetables, garnished with the parsley.

ADDING A LITTLE BIT OF BACON TO THIS CELERY DISH COULD BE SEEN AS A EUROPEAN APPROACH – BUT IT'S NOT DISSIMILAR TO HOW THEY COOK IN CHINA, TOO. THE CHINESE ARE EXTRAORDINARY IN THEIR CLEVER USE OF A SMALL AMOUNT OF MEAT TO FLAVOUR ENTIRE DISHES. I THINK THAT USING A LITTLE BIT OF MEAT OR BACON IS WORTHWHILE IF IT GETS PEOPLE WHO DON'T LIKE VEGIES TO EAT THEM!

# exercise to feel good

I believe you exercise to feel good and be healthier, not to watch your weight. And that if you want to lose weight or maintain your current weight, it's all in the kitchen.

It's interesting how much exercise is needed to burn off the simplest foods, let alone thosethat we know are unhealthy for us. Being able to cut a few calories from a meal is the equivalent of doing a session at the gym. For example, did you know that a medium banana, which has approximately 440 kilojoules, would take you ten minutes of active aerobics to burn off? One potato would take sixteen minutes of walking, and a bagel would take about twenty-three minutes of jogging. When you look at the amount of exercise needed to burn off food, you can see how important diet is.

But – keep exercising for a healthy, balanced lifestyle. I find I function much better through the day after I have done some weights at the gym or gone for a walk.

# BROOME VIETNAMESE SALAD

serves 4

This salad originated at a friend's house in Broome when I was wondering what to make from random ingredients in the kitchen. It has evolved over the years, and is a dish I always get asked to make. Take it to a friend's party and you'll be the star. It is excellent served with chicken.

## SALAD
100 g (2 cups) baby spinach leaves
200 g cherry tomatoes, halved
90 g (1 cup) bean sprouts
1 red onion, finely sliced
1 lemongrass stalk (white part only), finely chopped
1 kaffir lime leaf, finely shredded
½ cup coriander leaves
¼ cup vietnamese mint leaves, torn
sea salt
freshly ground black pepper
3 tablespoons cashews, roasted and chopped

## DRESSING
1 avocado
1 tablespoon olive oil
1 tablespoon lime juice
3 tablespoons Nahm Jim (page 22)

To make the dressing, put the avocado flesh, oil and lime juice in a food processor and blend until smooth. Transfer to a bowl and stir in the nahm jim.

Combine the spinach, cherry tomatoes, bean sprouts, onion, lemongrass, kafirr lime leaf, coriander and mint in a large bowl. Season with salt and pepper and add the dressing. Toss well. tServe garnished with the chopped cashews.

# ROASTED PUMPKIN AND HAZELNUT SALAD

serves 4–6

This is a really no-fuss, simple salad – something you can turn to when you're having an everyone's-here-in-an-hour-and-I-haven't-started-cooking emergency. I make it once a week and usually grill some chicken or fish or sometimes beef to have with it. You could also scatter it with some fresh goat's cheese for a good picnic dish or light lunch. My favourite types of pumpkin to use are butternut or blue.

800 g pumpkin, peeled and cut into
   2 cm cubes
1 red onion, quartered
2 tablespoons olive oil
sea salt
freshly ground black pepper
1 tablespoon lemon juice
200 g (4 cups) baby spinach leaves
¾ cup hazelnuts, roasted and roughly chopped

Preheat the oven to 220°C. Put the pumpkin and onion in a large baking dish and drizzle with 1 tablespoon of the oil. Season with salt and pepper and toss well. Roast for 40 minutes or until golden brown, then leave to cool to warm or to room temperature, depending on your preference. (In winter I like to serve the salad warm, while in summer I serve it cool.)

Meanwhile, make the dressing by combining the remaining oil with the lemon juice in a small bowl.

Tip the roasted pumpkin and onion into a large bowl and add the spinach, hazelnuts and dressing. Toss to combine, and serve.

NUTS ARE ONE OF THE BEST PLANT SOURCES OF PROTEIN AND ARE HIGH IN FIBRE AND ANTIOXIDANTS SUCH AS VITAMIN E AND SELENIUM. YES, THEY DO CONTAIN FAT, BUT IT'S MONOUNSATURATED AND POLYUNSATURATED FATS, INCLUDING OMEGA-3 FATTY ACIDS. THERE ARE VARIOUS CLAIMS AS TO WHICH NUTS ARE THE HEALTHIEST, BUT WALNUTS AND ALMONDS ARE JUST ABOUT ALWAYS AT THE TOP OF THE LIST. ALMONDS ARE VERY HIGH IN MAGNESIUM AND CALCIUM, WHILE WALNUTS ARE AN EXCELLENT SOURCE OF OMEGA-3, RIVALLING FISH. BUYING NATURAL RAW NUTS IS ALWAYS PREFERABLE TO ROASTED NUTS OR ONES DRENCHED IN SALT, SUGAR OR ARTIFICIAL FLAVOURINGS.

# CAULIFLOWER COUSCOUS

~~~~~~~~~~~~~~~~~~~~~~~~~

*serves 6*

The cauliflower is the couscous in this recipe, and it is raw too, making it a great way to enjoy the nutrition of raw food. (Cauliflower is actually my least-favourite vegetable when cooked, but raw it is surprisingly good!) This is a perfect side dish for a summer barbecue.

2 cauliflowers, broken into small florets
185 ml olive oil
3 tablespoons lemon juice
½ small red onion, finely chopped
100 g (¾ cup) pitted Spanish black olives, roughly
   chopped
18 sundried tomatoes, roughly chopped
¼ cup flat-leaf parsley leaves
¼ cup mint leaves
¼ cup coriander leaves
sea salt
freshly ground black pepper

Use a stick blender with a jug attachment to blend the cauliflower to the consistency of couscous. (You can try this with a food processor, but be very careful it doesn't grind it too smoothly.)

Put the cauliflower into a large bowl and add the oil, lemon juice, onion, olives, tomatoes and herbs. Season well with salt and pepper and toss to combine.

The way I approach preparing a meal is always very vegetable-oriented. Vegetables are the key for me – they are low in fat and calories, have a high nutritional content (brimming with vitamins, minerals and antioxidants), and are full of fibre, which keeps us feeling fuller for longer. Vegetables should always be the biggest portion on our plates in comparison to protein, carbohydrates and fats – but they do need to taste good. I believe that you shouldn't force yourself to eat vegetables because you're supposed to, but instead look for ways to make them delicious so that you want to eat them. Vegetable-based meals should be just as satisfying as ones containing meat.

I have a vegetarian dinner around one night a week – and at least half of my lunches are vegetarian. If you start with good produce, you are on your way to creating tasty dishes. I prefer to cook with organic produce as it contains more nutrients and is not sprayed with chemical fertilisers and pesticides – but I know this isn't an option for everyone all the time. I also like to support local growers as it is good for the local economy, ensures what you are eating is in season and at its peak, and cuts down on food miles. So even if it may cost a little more, I think the long-term benefits of buying local and organic – for the environment and for your health – are hard to ignore. If you're not sure where to get local organic produce, check the internet for listings.

The other option is of course growing some of your own vegetables! It's possible to do this even in a planter box on a balcony. Each season I try and grow something I've never grown before – and I look forward to reaping the rewards of the harvest.

# VEG

# ETAR

# IAN

# QUINOA PORRIDGE WITH SPICE AND BERRIES

*serves 4*

Breakfast is the one meal of the day that I base on carbohydrates, and for me this is usually oats. I am a big fan of porridge in winter, but too much of anything can get a little boring after a while. Using quinoa is a great alternative as it is packed with essential nutrients and has the flavour and filling qualities of a grain, even though it's actually a seed in the spinach family.

500 ml milk
1 teaspoon ground cinnamon
1 cardamom pod, seeds extracted
   from husk
1 teaspoon honey
2 cups quinoa

1 cup raspberries
1 cup blueberries
1 cup blackberries
3 tablespoons pistachios, roughly chopped

Put the milk, cinnamon, cardamom seeds and honey in a medium saucepan and bring to the boil. Reduce the heat to a simmer and add the quinoa. Cook for 40 minutes, or until the quinoa is tender.

Combine the berries and pistachios in a bowl. Serve the quinoa topped with the berries and nuts.

QUINOA (PRONOUNCED 'KEEN-WAH') REMAINS SLIGHTLY CRUNCHY WHEN COOKED AND HAS A WHOLESOME, SUBTLE FLAVOUR. TRULY A SUPER FOOD, IT CONTAINS GOOD QUANTITIES OF ALL NINE AMINO ACIDS THAT OUR BODIES MUST OBTAIN THROUGH FOOD, MAKING IT A COMPLETE PROTEIN. IT IS ALSO GLUTEN-FREE AND RICH IN FIBRE, MAGNESIUM, MANGANESE AND COPPER, AND CONTAINS ZINC, CALCIUM, POTASSIUM AND IRON.

# COOL THAI CURRY SOUP

serves 4

This is a refreshing soup to enjoy cold on a hot day, and a good starter to an Asian main course. I like to serve it before the Chicken Tenderloin Skewers on page 120. By not cooking the soup but blending it in a food processor instead, the big, fresh flavours of the raw ingredients really come through.

1 litre coconut water
3 garlic cloves, roughly chopped
4 cm piece of ginger, peeled and roughly chopped
3 coriander roots, cleaned
80 ml lemon juice
3 tablespoons soy sauce
2 tablespoons olive oil

1 tablespoon curry powder
1 teaspoon ground turmeric
¼ cup coriander leaves
¼ cup mint leaves

Place all the ingredients except the coriander and mint leaves in a food processor and blend for 5-6 minutes, or until smooth. Leave in the food processor for 10 minutes to allow the foam to settle on top. Use a large spoon to skim off the foam. Ladle into serving bowls and garnish with the coriander and mint.

COCONUT WATER – THE CLEAR LIQUID INSIDE A YOUNG COCONUT – IS, STRANGELY ENOUGH, THE CLOSEST THING TO THE PLASMA IN OUR BLOOD. IT HAS VIRTUALLY NO FAT OR SUGAR AND HAS A LOW GI, AS WELL AS BEING REFRESHING AND HYDRATING DUE TO ITS ELECTROLYTE CONTENT.

VEGETARIAN

# FIELD MUSHROOMS WITH NUT STUFFING AND GOAT'S CHEESE

*serves 6*

A tiny amount of good-quality goat's cheese goes a long way in this recipe. The stuffing is very easy to make and has crunch and depth of flavour with the combination of nuts, gremolata and thyme.

½ cup brazil nuts, finely chopped
½ cup cashews, finely chopped
½ cup macadamias, finely chopped
50 g (½ cup) almond meal
4 tablespoons Gremolata (page 22)
2 teaspoons thyme leaves

4 tablespoons lemon juice
sea salt
freshly ground black pepper
3 large field mushrooms
2 tablespoons fresh goat's cheese

Preheat the oven to 180°C. Line an oven tray with baking paper.

Combine the nuts, almond meal, gremolata, thyme and 2 table-spoons of the lemon juice in a bowl and mix well. Season with salt and pepper. Fill the mushrooms with the nut mixture and place on the tray. Crumble over small pieces of the goat's cheese and sprinkle with the remaining lemon juice. Bake in the oven f or 20-25 minutes, or until golden.

I LOVE MUSHROOMS. THEY ARE REALLY GOOD FOR YOU, BEING A GREAT SOURCE OF POTASSIUM, RIBOFLAVIN, NIACIN AND SELENIUM. THEY ARE ALSO GREAT TO INCORPORATE INTO YOUR DIET IF YOU ARE TRYING TO WATCH YOUR WEIGHT, AS THEY CONTAIN ABOUT EIGHTY TO NINETY PER CENT WATER AND ARE VERY LOW IN CALORIES.

# snacking after exercise

After exercise, most of us actually overcompensate for what our bodies really need and look for the food that we should eat least, such as something to give us a sugar hit. I appreciate sugar cravings a lot. When I was doing intense swimming training and my body was exhausted, I always craved something very sweet to give me an energy hit. I have a natural sweet tooth, but have trained myself over time to go for something with a slow energy release that is better for recovery, and has more nutrition. Various nuts and berries are usually my answer.

Refraining my sugar cravings after exercise took time for me, but now I'm reaping the benefits of having more sustained energy levels.

You know how you're really good at giving relationship advice to other people but bad at giving it to yourself? Think about this in regards to the food you eat. You probably know how to eat well and treat your body with respect, but need to direct that knowledge to yourself.

# MUSHROOM RISOTTO WITH BARLEY

*serves 6*

Barley is a fantastic grain as it cooks in a similar way to arborio rice (although it takes a little longer) and has a similar texture, but it boosts the meal's fibre content as well as adding a host of other nutrients. Barley also gives the risotto a rich, nutty flavour.

25 g dried porcini mushrooms
1 litre boiling water
1 litre Vegetable Stock (page 16)
1 bay leaf
2 tablespoons olive oil
2 teaspoons butter

2 onions, finely chopped
4 garlic cloves, crushed
2 cups pearl barley
250 ml red wine
250 g button or swiss-brown mushrooms, sliced
2 tablespoons chopped flat-leaf parsley

Place the dried porcini mushrooms in a bowl and cover with the boiling water. Soak for 15–20 minutes, then drain and reserve the water.

Put the mushroom water, vegetable stock and bay leaf in a medium saucepan and bring to the boil, then reduce the heat to a gentle simmer.

Heat the oil and butter in a large heavy-based saucepan and add the onion. Fry for 2–3 minutes, until translucent. Add the garlic and porcini mushrooms and fry for another minute. Add the barley and stir until well combined, then add the red wine and boil for about 2 minutes, until evaporated. Stir in the sliced fresh mushrooms, then begin to gradually add the stock a ladle at a time. Stir in each ladle of stock and simmer until absorbed before adding the next. Continue to add stock until it is all used and the barley is tender (approximately 40–45 minutes). Stir through the parsley and serve.

BARLEY IS A BIT OF A WONDER GRAIN, BEING A FANTASTIC SOURCE OF FIBRE AND SELENIUM AND A GOOD SOURCE OF PHOSPHORUS, COPPER AND MANGANESE. THE KIND OF SOLUBLE FIBRE IT CONTAINS CALLED BETA GLUCAN (ALSO FOUND IN OATS) HAS BEEN FOUND TO BE PARTICULARLY EFFECTIVE IN LOWERING CHOLESTEROL.

# 'TASTES LIKE CHICKEN' SALAD

*serves 6*

You will be shocked that this salad has no chicken in it – you could swear there was. It is based on sunflower seeds, which are soaked in water until soft and take on a meaty texture not unlike tinned tuna in a sandwich. The 'chicken' element comes from the dried herbs – they make the salad taste like the stuffed roast chook your grandma used to make!

3 cups sunflower seeds
4 celery stalks, finely sliced
3 spring onions, finely sliced
3 tablespoons dried oregano
3 tablespoons dried thyme
3 tablespoons dried sage

DRESSING
½ cup macadamias
½ cup cashews
½ cup pine nuts
½ cup brazil nuts
500 ml coconut water
250 ml lemon juice
90 g (⅓ cup) wholegrain mustard
6 garlic cloves, crushed
2 tablespoons sea salt

Put the sunflower seeds in a large bowl, cover with cold water and leave to soak a for 4 hours. Drain and pat dry, then return to the dried bowl.

Combine the dressing ingredients in a food processor and blend until smooth. Add the celery, spring onion and dried herbs to the sunflower seeds. Pour on the dressing and toss well.

# RUSTIC TUSCAN BEANS

~~~~~~~~~~~~~~~~~~~~~~~~~~~

*serves 6*

This dish is one of simple flavours – a thick stew of cannellini beans and tomatoes, with balsamic vinegar to give a bit of a lift. I like to serve these beans with a green salad.

400 g dried cannellini beans, soaked overnight

3 tablespoons olive oil

2 teaspoons sea salt

1 bouquet garni made of 1 bay leaf, 4 parsley stalks and 2 thyme sprigs tied with string

3 garlic cloves

2 sage sprigs

sprig of rosemary

5 vine-ripened tomatoes, peeled and roughly chopped

1½ tablespoons balsamic vinegar

freshly ground black pepper

Drain and rinse the beans, then put them in a large saucepan with 1 tablespoon of the oil, the salt and bouquet garni. Cover with plenty of water and bring to the boil. Reduce the heat to a simmer and cook for 1¼ hours, or until the beans are tender. As the beans are cooking, skim off any foam that rises to the surface. Drain the cooked beans.

Meanwhile, gently heat the remaining oil, garlic cloves, sage and rosemary in a large saucepan for 4–5 minutes, allowing the garlic and herbs to infuse the oil. Remove the garlic and herbs. Add the tomato and simmer for 15–20 minutes. Add the beans and continue to cook for a further 20 minutes. Remove from the heat, stir in the vinegar and season to taste with extra salt and pepper.

# SILVERBEET AND SUNDRIED TOMATO FRITTATA

*serves 2*

To get a good start to the day, you need a good breakfast, and when I'm sick of having porridge I like to have something like this frittata. Of course, it also works as a high-protein side dish or lunch. Leftovers are brilliant for breakfast, lunch or dinner during the rest of the week.

For a non-vegetarian frittata, you can add some cooked shredded chicken with the basil and parmesan before grilling.

4 eggs plus 2 egg whites
3 tablespoons milk
1 tablespoon dijon mustard
1 tablespoon olive oil
1 leek, finely sliced
4 garlic cloves, crushed

6 silverbeet leaves (stems discarded), shredded
2 tablespoons apple-cider vinegar
8 sundried tomatoes, finely chopped
1 tablespoon small basil leaves
80 g parmesan, grated

Combine the eggs and egg whites, milk and mustard in a medium bowl and whisk until just combined. Set aside.

Heat the olive oil in an ovenproof frying pan (around 20 cm in diameter) over medium heat. Add the leek and fry for 1–2 minutes, until starting to soften. Add the garlic and fry for another minute, then add the sliverbeet and vinegar, cover with a lid and cook for 5 minutes, or until the silverbeet has wilted. Scatter with the tomatoes and pour on the egg mixture. Continue to cook for 5–6 minutes, until the frittata is just beginning to set. Scatter with the basil leaves and parmesan. Transfer to a preheated grill and cook for 7–8 minutes, until golden. Cut into wedges and serve.

AN INTERESTING FACT ABOUT GARLIC IS THAT ITS MAJOR HEALTH-GIVING COMPONENT, ALLICIN, IS ONLY GENERATED WHEN YOU CHOP OR CRUSH IT. ALLICIN IS RESPONSIBLE FOR ITS STRONG ODOUR, AND HAS ANTIBIOTIC PROPERTIES THAT FIGHT A WIDE RANGE OF VIRUSES AND BACTERIA. EATING RAW GARLIC, SUCH AS CRUSHED IN SALAD DRESSINGS, GIVES YOU THE MOST BENEFITS.

# PARIPPU (DHAL)

~~~~~~~~~~~~~~~~~~~~~~~~~~~~

### serves 4

Parippu is a dhal from southern India or Sri Lanka. If you use my No-fat Coconut Milk on page 20, then this dish of protein-rich lentils is very good for you.

**DHAL**
1½ cups red lentils, rinsed
2 onions, roughly chopped
2 tomatoes, roughly chopped
2 long green chillies, finely sliced
2 teaspoons ground cumin
2 teaspoons ground coriander
1 teaspoon ground turmeric
500 ml Vegetable Stock (page 16)
250 ml No-fat Coconut Milk (page 20)

**TO FINISH**
2 tablespoons vegetable oil
1 teaspoon cumin seeds
1 teaspoon mustard seeds
2 onions, finely chopped
12 curry leaves

Place the dhal ingredients in a large heavy-based saucepan and bring to the boil. Reduce the heat and simmer for 30 minutes, or until the lentils are cooked.

Heat the oil in a frying pan over low–medium heat. Add the cumin and mustard seeds and fry for 1–2 minutes until they begin to pop. Add the onion and curry leaves and continue to fry for around 7–8 minutes until the onion is well browned. Stir the onion mixture through the lentils, then serve.

WHEN A RECIPE CALLS FOR GROUND SPICES, SUCH AS CUMIN AND CORIANDER, I LIKE TO ROAST AND GRIND MY OWN. I ROAST THEM IN A DRY FRYING PAN UNTIL FRAGRANT, THEN GRIND THEM WITH A MORTAR AND PESTLE. THERE'S NOTHING IN THE KITCHEN MORE PLEASURABLE THAN DRY-ROASTING SPICES, AND GETTING THE COMBINATIONS RIGHT IN A DISH CAN BE A LOT OF FUN. IT'S LIKE PLAYING CHEMIST – SEEING WHAT WORKS WITH A LITTLE BIT OF THIS AND A LITTLE BIT OF THAT.

# NORTH AFRICAN TOMATO AND GREEN LENTIL STEW

~~~~~~~~~~~~~~~~~~~~~~~~~~~~

*serves 10*

A large quantity of tomatoes is used in this dish, and they are roasted first with red onion and garlic to intensify their flavour. I think this makes a perfect lunch – nothing else required.

3.5 kg tomatoes, chopped
2 red onions, sliced
4 garlic cloves
2 tablespoons sugar
1 tablespoon ground cumin
80 ml olive oil
sea salt
freshly ground black pepper
2 cups green lentils

3 cm piece of ginger, peeled
1 bay leaf
2 litres Vegetable Stock (page 16)
250 ml tomato puree
3 tablespoons tomato paste
1 teaspoon sweet paprika
flat-leaf parsley leaves
Harissa (page 20) to serve

Preheat the oven to 180°C. Put the tomato, onion and garlic in a large baking dish. Sprinkle with the sugar and cumin and drizzle with the olive oil. Season with salt and pepper and toss well. Bake for about 1 hour, until well browned.

Meanwhile, place the lentils, ginger, bay leaf and stock in a large saucepan and bring to the boil. Reduce the heat and simmer for 35–40 minutes, or until the lentils are tender. Remove the ginger and bay leaf.

Stir the tomato and onion mixture into the lentils, along with the tomato puree, tomato paste and paprika. Season to taste. Serve garnished with parsley leaves, with harissa on the side.

# VIETNAMESE TOFU AND
# VEGETABLE STIR-FRY

~~~~~~~~~~~~~~~~~~~~~~~~~~

## serves 4

This stir-fry is flavoured with kaffir lime and coriander root, and makes a great light lunch. It can also be served as a side dish.

2 tablespoons peanut oil
300 g firm tofu, cut into 3 cm cubes
1 long red chilli, sliced
2 kaffir lime leaves, finely shredded
2 coriander roots, cleaned and finely chopped
1 bunch choy sum, cut into 3 cm lengths
½ red capsicum, sliced
50 g button mushrooms, sliced
1 punnet (125 g) baby corn, halved lengthwise
2 tablespoons soy sauce

Heat the oil in a wok over medium heat. Add the tofu cubes and fry for 1–2 minutes on each side, until browned all over. Transfer to a plate, leaving some oil in the wok.

Add the chilli, lime leaves and coriander root to the wok and stir-fry for 1–2 minutes, until fragrant. Add the choy sum stems and capsicum and stir-fry for 2–3 minutes, then add the mushrooms, corn, choy sum leaves and soy sauce and stir-fry for another 2–3 minutes, until the vegetables are tender. Gently toss the tofu through the vegetables and serve.

IF YOU KNOW WHAT GOES INTO YOUR MEAL, YOU KNOW WHAT GOES INTO YOUR BODY. I DON'T COOK WITH PREMADE SAUCES OR FLAVOUR PACKETS AS THERE IS OFTEN A LOT OF SUGAR, SALT AND FAT IN THEM. THESE ARE THINGS I'D PREFER TO ADD MYSELF WITHOUT OVERDOING IT.

# BOOM BOOM POW (INDIAN MUSHROOMS AND BLACK-EYED BEANS)

serves 4

'Boom Boom Pow' is a song by the Black-Eyed Peas, and I think it's a good name for this dish. Black-eyed peas – or black-eyed beans – are a source of protein, calcium, folate and vitamin A, but you don't need to cook this just because it is healthy. Aromatic with cumin and cinnamon, it is also delicious. It can be served as part of an Indian banquet or on its own.

200 g dried black-eyed beans, soaked overnight
1 bay leaf
3 tablespoons olive oil
1 tablespoon cumin seeds
1 cinnamon stick
3 medium onions, finely chopped
4 garlic cloves, crushed
400 g button mushrooms, sliced
800 g tin of diced tomatoes

3 teaspoons ground coriander
2 teaspoons ground cumin
1 teaspoon ground turmeric
1 teaspoon ground cinnamon
1 teaspoon cayenne pepper
¼ cup coriander leaves
sea salt
freshly ground black pepper

Drain the beans and put them in a saucepan with the bay leaf. Cover with fresh water and bring to the boil, then reduce the heat to a simmer and cook for 20–25 minutes, until the beans are tender. Drain the beans and remove the bay leaf.

While the beans are cooking, heat the oil in a large heavy-based saucepan and add the cumin seeds and cinnamon stick. Fry for 1 minute, until the cumin seeds begin to pop. Add the onion and garlic and fry for 2–3 minutes, until starting to brown. Add the mushrooms and fry for another 2–3 minutes, then add the tomato and ground spices. Cover with a lid and simmer for 10 minutes.

Stir in the beans and coriander leaves and season with salt and pepper, then cook for another 30 minutes.

There should be a rule that as your palate matures, you have to retry everything you didn't like when you were a kid. I absolutely love tuna now, but I remember when I was young, being made to eat Mum's tuna mornay and hating it. I didn't like seafood in general – in fact, when I was growing up, I didn't like half the things I love now. For me, it's a reminder to never assume you don't like something, and to retry things at different stages of your life, and perhaps try them in new ways.

Now I appreciate fish and seafood for their health benefits as well as their flavour. They are high in quality protein and fats and contains minerals such as iodine, zinc, magnesium, potassium and phosphorus, and vitamins A, E, C and D. Some of the benefits of eating fish regularly include boosting the immune system and maintaining healthy, glowing skin.

The Omega-3 fatty acids found in fish and seafood are one of their greatest claims to fame, as this polyunsaturated fat can lower cholesteroland blood pressure and decrease the risk of heart disease, and has also been found to be beneficial in preventing osteoporosis and treating rheumatoid arthritis.

One of my favourite fish to cook is barramundi, as it has a delicate flavour that lends itself to many dishes. I also cook with salmon as, particularly rich in Omega-3, I know how good it is for me.

# SEA
# FOOD

# MISO COD

serves 4

Nobu is one of my favourite restaurants, especially the one in New York where I first ate one of their signature dishes – miso black cod. Since then I've eaten similar dishes in my travels to Japan. My recipe has less sugar than most, and uses blue-eye trevalla (also known as blue-eye cod).

The fish is coated in a miso marinade and left in the refrigerator for two or three days, so I think you should befriend your fishmonger to make sure the fish is really fresh. The fish is then pan-fried and it emerges tasting as if it has been smothered in butter – a magical trick worked by the miso, but with no reason to feel guilty afterwards. I prefer to serve the fish on its own as a main course to let it really feature, but I start with something green and healthy. White miso is the kind I normally use, although the recipe will work with any miso.

125 ml mirin
3 tablespoons sake
400 g (1½ cups) miso
150 g (²/₃ cup) sugar
4 x 220 g blue-eye trevalla fillets,
    skin on

Put the mirin and sake in a small saucepan and bring to the boil. Reduce the heat to a simmer and add the miso and sugar. Stir until dissolved, then remove from the heat and leave to cool. Set aside 3 tablespoons of the mixture in a small bowl to use as a dressing.

Lay the fish fillets in a shallow dish and cover completely with the miso mixture. Cover with plastic wrap and refrigerate along with the bowl of dressing for 2 or 3 days.

Preheat the oven to 220°C. Heat a frying pan over medium heat. Remove the fish from the marinade and add it to the pan, skin-side down. Fry for 3 minutes, then turn and cook for another 3 minutes. Transfer to an oven tray and bake for 8–10 minutes, or until cooked to your liking. Serve drizzled with the reserved miso dressing.

IT'S ALL ABOUT COMMUNICATION WHEN IT COMES TO BUYING FOOD. IT'S ABOUT SPEAKING TO SOMEONE WHO KNOWS MORE THAN YOU DO ABOUT WHAT YOU'RE BUYING – IT WILL PROBABLY BE YOUR LOCAL BUTCHER, GREENGROCER OR FISHMONGER. YOU KNOW YOU'VE GOT A GOOD RELATIONSHIP WHEN YOU CAN WALK INTO A SHOP AND SAY 'WHAT'S GOOD TODAY?'

# MRS JOYCE'S LEBANESE FISH

*serves 4*

Mrs Joyce is my friend Bec's mum, and her fantastic fish recipe is one you just can't get wrong. Due to the big flavours of lots of red onions and balsamic vinegar, you don't have to use a premium fish, which is always good for the budget. Serve the dish with a green salad.

2 tablespoons olive oil
6 red onions, finely sliced
80 ml balsamic vinegar
sea salt
freshly ground black pepper
4 x 200 g skinless blue grenadier fillets

Heat the oil in a heavy-based saucepan over low heat. Add the onion and cook, stirring occasionally, for 1 hour, until very soft. Stir in the vinegar and season with salt and pepper. Allow to cool a little.

Preheat the oven to 180°C. Lay the fish in a baking dish and top with the onion. Cover with foil and bake for 7 minutes, then remove the foil and bake for another 7 minutes.

IT'S FANTASTIC TO REALISE THAT A COMMON INGREDIENT LIKE THE ONION IS SO GOOD FOR YOU. ONIONS ARE A GREAT SOURCE OF FLAVONOIDS, WHICH ARE COMPOUNDS WITH ANTIOXIDANT EFFECTS FOUND IN PLANT FOODS. ONE MAJOR FLAVONOID IN ONIONS, QUERCETIN, HELPS TO PROTECT AGAINST CARDIOVASCULAR DISEASE, IS ANTI-INFLAMMATORY, AND RELIEVES ALLERGY SYMPTOMS. RED ONIONS HAVE MORE QUERCETIN THAN WHITE ONIONS, AND MOST IS LOCATED CLOSE TO THE SKIN OF THE ONION SO THEY SHOULDN'T BE OVER-PEELED. ONIONS ALSO CONTAIN VITAMIN C AND THE MINERAL CHROMIUM, WHICH ASSISTS IN CONTROLLING BLOOD-SUGAR LEVELS.

# getting cooking tips on my travels

One of the things I try to do with my cooking is bring in all the influences from my travels around the world. So, I have taken what I have experienced and liked, and what fits in with a healthy and realistic lifestyle, and integrated it into the food I cook and the way I eat. When I was in Tuscany I loved how almost everything they served came out of the garden and was seasonal and fresh. And when I go to Japan, I always notice how the quality rather than the quantity of food is paramount, and that meals always consist of great variety.

# BARRAMUNDI WITH PRESERVED LEMON, TOMATO AND PINE NUTS

*serves 4*

For this dish I use the flesh of preserved lemon rather than the usual skin, as it has a sweet, subtle flavour that doesn't overpower the wonderful barramundi. Serve the fish and sauce with wilted baby spinach leaves.

3 tablespoons olive oil
1 tomato, finely chopped
½ preserved lemon, flesh only, finely chopped
1 tablespoon pine nuts, toasted
2 tablespoons lemon juice
1 tablespoon finely chopped flat-leaf parsley
1 teaspoon finely chopped thyme
1 teaspoon finely chopped oregano
4 x 150 g barramundi fillets, skin on

Heat 2 tablespoons of the oil in a small saucepan and add the tomato, preserved lemon, pine nuts, lemon juice and herbs. Cook for 2–3 minutes, then remove from the heat.

While the sauce is cooking, heat the remaining oil in a large frying pan. Cook the fish skin-side down for 3–4 minutes, until crisp. Turn the fish and cook for another 2 minutes, or until cooked to your liking. Serve the fish topped with the warm sauce.

# BEETROOT-CURED SALMON
# WITH FENNEL SALAD

~~~~~~~~~~~~~~~~~~~~~~~~~~~~~~~~~~~~~~~~~~

*serves 6*

This dish can make you appear a more expert cook than you really are! Everyone always tries to guess what flavours are in it. The fennel seeds give the dish fresh earthiness, while the beetroot gives it sweetness as well as vibrant colour.

2 tablespoons black peppercorns
1 tablespoon fennel seeds
4 beetroots, peeled and grated
2 limes, zested and juiced
1 orange, zested and juiced
1 cup dill leaves, finely chopped
1 cup flat-leaf parsley leaves, finely chopped
330 g (1½ cups) caster sugar
130 g (1 cup) sea salt
1.2 kg side of salmon, pin-boned and skinned

**FENNEL SALAD**
2 baby fennel bulbs, finely sliced
1 red onion, finely sliced
1 cup mache leaves (lamb's lettuce)
¼ cup dill leaves, chopped
2 tablespoons lemon juice
freshly ground black pepper

Finely grind the peppercorns and fennel seeds in a mortar. Transfer to a bowl along with the beetroot, citrus zest and juice, herbs, sugar and salt and toss well.

Place the salmon in a large, deep tray and cover the top with the beetroot mix. Cover and refrigerate for 24 hours. Turn the salmon and re-cover with the beetroot mix, and refrigerate for a further 12 hours.

To make the salad, combine the fennel, onion, mache and dill in a bowl. Dress with the lemon juice, season with pepper and toss to combine.

Scrape the beetroot mixture from the salmon and pat the fish dry. Finely slice the fish and serve with the fennel salad.

BEETROOT IS AS HEALTHY AS IT IS COLOURFUL, WITH STUDIES SHOWING THAT IT LOWERS CHOLESTEROL AND BLOOD PRESSURE AND EVEN BOOSTS ENDURANCE BY MAKING THE BODY'S UPTAKE OF OXYGEN MORE EFFICIENT. ONE ANTIOXIDANT THAT BEETROOT CONTAINS CALLED BETACYANIN – WHICH IS ALSO THE PIGMENT RESPONSIBLE FOR ITS DEEP RED COLOUR – HAS BEEN SHOWN TO PREVENT CANCERS SUCH AS COLON CANCER.

# SQUID, BLOOD ORANGE, POMEGRANATE AND FENNEL SALAD

serves 4

This salad is packed with antioxidants from the pomegranate and blood oranges – and I guarantee it will make a good impression when entertaining. It makes me think of summer in Italy!

2 blood oranges
2 teaspoons sea salt
2 teaspoons freshly ground black pepper
500 g squid tubes, quartered lengthwise and finely scored
1 fennel bulb, finely sliced
seeds of 1 pomegranate
250 g (4 cups) mixed salad leaves

DRESSING
2 tablespoons Campari
2 tablespoons juice reserved from segmenting the blood oranges
2 teaspoons orange-blossom water (instead you could use 1 teaspoon caster sugar)
3 tablespoons olive oil

Use a small, sharp knife to cut the peel from the oranges, making sure to remove all the white pith. Hold the oranges over a bowl to catch any juice and cut on either side of each segment to remove wedges of flesh, leaving the membranes behind. Drop the wedges into another bowl. Squeeze the juice from the membranes and measure out 2 tablespoons for the dressing.

To make the dressing, bring the Campari to the boil in a small saucepan. Reduce the heat and whisk in the juice, orange-blossom water and oil. Remove from the heat and leave to cool.

Preheat a barbecue grill to medium. Combine the salt and pepper on a plate. Toss the squid in the salt and pepper, then grill the pieces for 1–2 minutes on each side.

Combine the squid, blood-orange segments, fennel, pomegranate seeds and salad leaves in a bowl. Pour on the dressing and toss well.

POMEGRANATES CONTAIN THREE TIMES THE AMOUNT OF ANTIOXIDANTS FOUND IN GREEN TEA – WHICH IS ITSELF A WELL-KNOWN POWERHOUSE OF ANTIOXIDANTS. AND, BLOOD ORANGES ARE RICH IN THE ANTIOXIDANT KNOWN AS ANTHOCYANIN.

# GRILLED SALMON WITH
# ROASTED RED CAPSICUM PESTO

~~~~~~~~~~~~~~~~~~~~

*serves 4*

The sweetness of the roasted capsicum works really well with the rich flavour of the salmon. This dish also looks beautiful with bursts of red and pink. Serve with steamed or chargrilled asparagus or Roasted Pumpkin and Hazelnut Salad (page 45).

### PESTO
2 red capsicums
¼ cup macadamias
1 ½ tablespoons pine nuts
25 g parmesan, grated

4 x 120 g salmon fillets, skin on

Preheat a barbecue grill to high. Roast the capsicums on the grill until blackened all over (about 20–30 minutes). Place in a deep bowl, cover with plastic wrap and leave to steam and cool for 15 minutes, then peel and seed the capsicums.

Put the capsicum flesh, macadamias, pine nuts and parmesan in a food processor and blend until smooth.

Preheat the barbecue grill once more, and preheat your oven grill. Grill the salmon on the barbecue skin-side down for 2–3 minutes until just golden. Transfer the fillets, skin-side down, to an oven tray, spoon over the capsicum pesto and cook under the oven grill for 2–3 minutes, or until cooked to your liking.

SALMON REALLY IS A SUPERSTAR OF THE FISH WORLD DUE TO ITS HIGH NUTRITIONAL VALUE. IT IS A GREAT SOURCE OF VITAMINS B6 AND B12, AND THE MINERALS PHOSPHORUS, NIACIN AND MAGNESIUM. SALMON IS ALSO HIGH IN PROTEIN AND – PERHAPS MOST IMPORTANTLY OF ALL – IN OMEGA-3 FATTY ACIDS THAT ARE ESSENTIAL TO OUR BODY'S FUNCTION.

I AM ACTUALLY A FAIRLY AVERAGE FISHERMAN
BUT I NOTICED A NEIGHBOUR CATCHING SQUID
ONE DAY AND HE TOLD ME HOW TO DO IT. IT'S A
LOT EASIER THAN YOU MIGHT THINK. I USUALLY
GO ONCE A WEEK, AND THE RESULT IS PLENTY OF
FRESH SQUID FOR EVERYONE AT MY HOUSE

# PAD THAI WITH SQUID 'NOODLES'

*serves 4*

Pad Thai is normally made with flat rice noodles, but I like to cut my own 'noodles' from the squid. This brings down the carbohydrate content of the dish and adds the extra nutrition of seafood. Krachai, also known as lesser ginger, is a long, thin, finger-shaped rhizome that adds an earthy, authentic flavour to Thai dishes like this one. Look for it at Asian grocers – but if you can't find it, it can be omitted.

Don't let the long ingredients list intimidate you. The dish isn't hard to make – there's just a bit of chopping to get through, but then the cooking is quick. I like to make pad Thai when I have friends over and I can delegate some of the chopping to them!

120 ml vegetable oil

700 g squid tubes, opened out flat and finely sliced into 'noodles'

2 eggs

5 spring onions, finely sliced

2 tablespoons finely chopped garlic chives

2 tablespoons finely chopped coriander, plus extra leaves to serve

½ teaspoon dried chilli flakes

200 g pork fillet, finely sliced

300 g raw prawns, shelled and de-veined

6 small krachai (lesser ginger) fingers, peeled and sliced

3 garlic cloves, crushed

180 g (2 cups) bean sprouts, trimmed

3 tablespoons peanuts, roasted and chopped

sliced red chilli to serve

lime wedges to serve

### SAUCE

3 tablespoons tamarind puree

3 tablespoons fish sauce

3 tablespoons lemon juice

1½ tablespoons grated palm sugar

1 teaspoon Thai shrimp paste

To make the sauce, mash the ingredients together in a small bowl and set aside.

Heat a tablespoon of the oil in a wok over high heat. Add a third of the squid and fry for 2–3 minutes, until milky white. Transfer to paper towel to drain and continue cooking the remaining squid in two more batches, using a tablespoon of oil each time.

Lightly beat the eggs, spring onion, garlic chives, coriander and chilli flakes in a bowl and set aside. Heat the remaining oil in the wok over medium heat and stir-fry the pork for 2–4 minutes, until browned all over. Add the prawns, krachai and garlic and stir-fry for another 2 minutes, then add the sauce and cook for a further 2 minutes. Push all the ingredients to one side of the wok and pour in the egg mixture. Lightly scramble the egg as it begins to set, creating bite-sized pieces, then add the squid noodles, bean sprouts and peanuts and toss until well combined and heated through.

Serve with coriander leaves, sliced chilli and lime wedges.

# FISH AND PRAWNS IN COCONUT MILK AND RED PALM-FRUIT OIL

*serves 4*

This is a Brazilian seafood stew called *moqueca de peixe*. It is delicious served with steamed green vegetables, brown rice and a hot chilli sauce such as Tabasco. Red palm-fruit oil became popular in Brazilian cooking after African slaves arrived there.

500 g firm white fish fillets, cut into 3 cm chunks
500 g raw prawns, shelled and de-veined
sea salt
freshly ground black pepper
2 tablespoons olive oil
1 onion, finely chopped
2 tablespoons tomato paste

1 tomato, roughly chopped
2 red capsicums, finely chopped
250 ml coconut milk
1 tablespoon red palm-fruit oil
¼ cup coriander leaves
3 tablespoons cashews, roasted

Preheat the oven to 200°C. Season the fish and prawns with salt and pepper.

Heat the olive oil in a heavy-based ovenproof saucepan and add the onion. Fry for 5 minutes, until translucent, then add the tomato paste, fresh tomato and capsicum and cook for 10 minutes, until the capsicum is soft. Stir in the coconut milk, palm-fruit oil and 2 tablespoons of water, followed by the fish and prawns. Cover with a lid and transfer the pan to the oven for 10–15 minutes, or until the seafood is cooked through. Garnish with the coriander and cashews to serve.

THE OIL PALM ORIGINATES IN AFRICA, WHERE IT IS LARGELY A SUSTAINABLE PRODUCT MADE BY SMALL-SCALE FAMILY PRODUCERS. WHILE THE KERNEL INSIDE THE PALM FRUIT PRODUCES A COLOURLESS OIL VALUED FOR USE IN PRODUCTS SUCH AS SOAP, OIL FROM THE FRUIT ITSELF IS A RICH RED COLOUR AND IS VERY HIGH IN VITAMIN E AND BETA CAROTENE (WHICH OUR BODIES CONVERT TO VITAMIN A), AND IT HAS MORE MONOSATURATED (VERSUS SATURATED) FAT.

# ZUKE TUNA

serves 6 as an entree

'Zuke' is a Japanese word for marinate, and this is a great introduction to eating raw fish.

3 tablespoons mirin
3 tablespoons sake
3 tablespoons soy sauce
2 garlic cloves, crushed

1 small red chilli, seeded and finely sliced
1 cm piece of ginger, peeled and finely sliced
1 teaspoon grated palm sugar
150 g sashimi-grade tuna (from the belly)

To make the marinade, place the mirin and sake in a small saucepan and bring to the boil, then remove from the heat and add the soy sauce, garlic, chilli, ginger and palm sugar. Leave to cool.

Put the tuna in a bowl and coat with the marinade. Refrigerate overnight.

Bring a large saucepan of water to the boil. Remove the tuna from the marinade and wrap tightly in plastic wrap, securing the ends with rubber bands. Cook the tuna in the boiling water for 1-2 minutes – it should still be rare inside. When cool enough to handle, discard the plastic wrap and slice finely.

# CRAYFISH AND CRAB SUSHI

serves 6–8 as an entree

For me, this is a special-occasion dish – not just because of the crayfish and crab, but also the white sushi rice. It works really well as an appetiser for a dinner party.

1 medium cooked crayfish
145 g cooked crab meat
½ cup Japanese mayonnaise
freshly ground black pepper

4 nori sheets
4 cups cooked sushi rice
  (page 23)
1 cup dukkah

Remove the crayfish tail meat from its shell – you don't need the legs for the sushi so you can enjoy them separately. Finely chop the crayfish and crab meat, then combine them in a bowl with the mayonnaise. Season well with pepper.

Cover a sushi mat with plastic wrap so the rice doesn't stick to it. Place a sheet of nori on the mat. Wet your hands and add a large handful of rice in the middle of the nori and start spreading it out gently until about 1 cm thick and even across the nori sheet (add more rice if you don't have enough). Turn the nori and rice over so that the rice is facing down onto the plastic. Spread a quarter of the crayfish and crab mixture along one long edge of the nori sheet. Use the mat to roll the rice and nori over the filling gently but firmly. Continue rolling up, keeping the roll tight.

Scatter the dukkah over a board or work surface and roll the rice roll in dukkah until well coated. Set the roll aside and continue making rolls from the remaining nori sheets, rice and crayfish and crab mixture, rolling them in dukkah. Use a wet sharp knife to cut each roll into 6-8 pieces.

# OYSTERS IN SEVEN DEADLY SINS

*serves 6*

These oysters are great for a dinner party and a fun way to kick off an evening – get everyone to choose their favourite sin.

## PASSION
Nahm Jim (page 22)
6 oysters

Spoon a little nahm jim onto each oyster.

## GLUTTONY
3 slices of prosciutto, finely sliced crosswise
3 tablespoons worcestershire sauce
6 oysters

Top the oysters with the prosciutto and spoon over half the worcestershire. Cook under a hot grill for 2–3 minutes until the prosciutto is crisp. Spoon over the rest of the worcestershire.

## GREED
120 ml champagne
1½ tablespoons butter
6 oysters

Heat the champagne and butter in a small saucepan, stirring until the butter melts and the mixture is well combined. Spoon over the oysters.

## AVARICE
3 shallots, finely chopped
3 tablespoons balsamic vinegar
6 oysters

Combine the shallots and vinegar and spoon over the oysters.

## ENVY
3 kaffir lime leaves, very finely shredded
3 teaspoons vodka
6 oysters

Combine the lime leaves and vodka and spoon over the oysters.

## WRATH
small knob of ginger, peeled and grated
8 cm piece of cucumber, very finely chopped
3 teaspoons red-wine vinegar
6 oysters

Combine the ginger, cucumber and vinegar and spoon over the oysters.

## SLOTH
Serve the oysters natural – 'sloth' translates as 'can't be bothered'!

OYSTERS MAKE A GREAT 'SEVEN DEADLY SINS' DISH AS THEY ARE QUITE FAMOUS FOR BEING AN APHRODISIAC. THIS IS BECAUSE THEY ARE RICH IN AMINO ACIDS AND ZINC, WHICH ARE IMPORTANT FOR TESTOSTERONE PRODUCTION, FERTILITY, REPRODUCTIVE HEALTH AND LIBIDO. OYSTERS ARE ALSO RICH IN IRON, CALCIUM AND VITAMIN A.

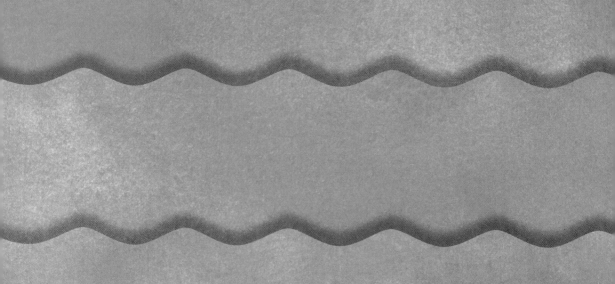

Whether roasted, grilled or turned into a curry or a stir-fry, chicken is such a versatile meat to cook, and a bit of a no-brainer for many of us when it comes to preparing a quick and tasty meal. I love to cook and eat chicken as much as the next person, although I do like to cook other poultry as well, such as quail and turkey.

Turkey is something many of us only consider eating at Christmas, but it deserves to be more widely enjoyed! I would like to encourage people to sometimes try turkey tenderloin as a replacement for chicken breast as it's lower in fat and higher in protein. I like the fact that it can be used in most dishes where you would use chicken breast, but it has a different taste, so it adds variety to your meals.

Along with other meats, poultry is a good source of iron, zinc, B vitamins and other nutrients — such as selenium, which helps support the immune system. Environmentally, it is better than red meat (some of the reasons are the smaller amount of farmland required and less methane expelled by the animals), so I try to eat a little more sustainably and reduce my red meat consumption to two meals per week and have poultry or fish more often. I usually have two meals of poultry a week, and the same for fish. I also make an effort to buy free-range and certified organic poultry, as not only are the animals raised in a healthier and happier way, but the meat has more nutrients and no contaminants.

# POU
# LTRY

# THREE-DAY CHICKEN

*serves 4*

I love this dish so much that I make it every two weeks. It features chicken poached in stock, then shredded and coated in a sweet medieval-flavoured dressing with raisins, citrus zest and cinnamon. The chicken is left to marinate in the dressing for three days, then it is tossed with an extravagant amount of pine nuts, parsley and olive oil.

When you are entertaining, you don't want to spend all your time in the kitchen, which is why having a dish like this one that can be prepared ahead (a long way in this case!) is really handy.

1.8 kg free-range chicken
1.5 litres Chicken Stock (page 15)
2 cups pine nuts, toasted
½ cup flat-leaf parsley leaves, chopped
80–250 ml olive oil

DRESSING

1 orange
1 lemon
125 ml red-wine vinegar
2 bay leaves
2 tablespoons sugar
1 cinnamon stick
½ teaspoon freshly ground black pepper
1 cup raisins

Place the chicken in a large saucepan and cover with the stock. Bring to the boil, then reduce the heat to a simmer and skim off any foam or impurities that have risen to the surface. Simmer the chicken with the lid off for 45 minutes, then remove the chicken from the stock and set aside to cool. Reserve the stock for other recipes.

To make the dressing, use a vegetable peeler to peel the zest from the orange and lemon, then slice it finely. You don't need the remaining orange and lemon for this recipe.

Put the red-wine vinegar, bay leaves, sugar and cinnamon stick in a saucepan and bring to a simmer. Cook for 10 minutes, then add the pepper, raisins and orange and lemon zest and continue cooking for a further 10 minutes. Remove from the heat and set aside to cool.

Remove the skin from the cooled chicken and discard. Shred the meat into small bite-sized pieces. Put the meat in a ceramic or glass bowl and pour over the dressing. Cover with plastic wrap and refrigerate for 2–3 days.

To serve, toss the pine nuts and parsley through the chicken and dress with olive oil to taste.

# CARDAMOM CHICKEN

*serves 4*

Not all Indian food needs to be hot. This is a mild chicken curry spiked with cardamom and lemon zest, and it also has eight green chillies, but they are pricked with a skewer and added whole to add flavour without too much heat at all.

20 cardamom pods, seeds extracted from husks

2 teaspoons black peppercorns

250 ml natural yoghurt

4 garlic cloves

4 cm peice of ginger, peeled and roughly chopped

1 tablespoon grated lemon zest

1.5 kg free-range chicken, cut into 8 pieces

2 tablespoons olive oil

400 ml coconut milk

8 long green chillies, each pricked around 10 times with a skewer

¼ cup coriander leaves, roughly chopped

3 tablespoons lemon juice

sea salt

Put the cardamom seeds and peppercorns in a mortar and grind to a powder. Add 2 tablespoons of the yoghurt along with the garlic, ginger and lemon zest and grind to a paste. Rub the paste all over the chicken pieces and marinate in the refrigerator overnight.

Heat the oil in a large frying pan over medium-high heat. Add the chicken pieces and cook for 2–3 minutes on each side, until browned. Add the remaining yoghurt, coconut milk and chillies and simmer gently for 25–30 minutes, until the chicken is cooked through. Add the coriander, lemon juice and salt to taste.

CARDAMOM IS NATIVE TO SOUTHERN INDIA AND HAS BEEN USED IN INDIAN COOKING FOR THOUSANDS OF YEARS. THE PODS ARE ACTUALLY THE DRIED FRUITS OF A TROPICAL PLANT IN THE GINGER FAMILY, AND EACH ONE CONTAINS UP TO TWENTY STICKY BLACK OR BROWN SEEDS THAT HAVE A STRONG, FRUITY FRAGRANCE. CARDAMOM SEEDS LOSE THEIR FLAVOUR WHEN EXPOSED TO AIR, SO IT IS BEST TO BUY PODS AND GRIND THE SEEDS AS NEEDED.

# low-fat labels

I don't agree with extremes. I think 'low fat' is extreme and not sustainable, and also contradictory. As lollies are low fat, can we eat a lot of lollies? No. Labels proclaiming low or reduced fat send the message that it's okay to eat something because the label says so, but unfortunately 'low fat' can often disguise a high sugar or salt content.

# SPICY QUAIL BREASTS WITH SHALLOT 'BUTTER'

*serves 4*

You can buy quail breasts at some good-quality butchers and they are worth seeking out, being so much more convenient than boning them out yourself!

My rule for this dish is that you must make it with two chillies so it is nice and spicy. The 'butter' is actually made of yoghurt, which always helps to cool things down. The dish is delicious served with Chilli Coleslaw (page 160).

4 garlic cloves, crushed
2 long red chillies, finely chopped
1 tablespoon olive oil
1 tablespoon soy sauce
1 teaspoon cayenne pepper
½ teaspoon ground cinnamon
½ teaspoon ground cloves
16 (600 g) quail breasts, skin on

### SHALLOT 'BUTTER'

4 shallots, roughly chopped
¼ cup flat-leaf parsley leaves
2 tablespoons natural yoghurt
1 tablespoon lemon juice

Combine the garlic, chilli, oil, soy sauce and spices in a large bowl and mix together. Stir in the quail breasts, coating them well, and marinate in the refrigerator overnight.

Put the ingredients for the shallot butter in a food processor and blend until smooth. Transfer to a bowl and refrigerate until ready to use.

Preheat an oven grill to medium. Place the quail breasts, skin-side up, on an oven tray and grill for 5–6 minutes, until golden brown. Serve topped with the shallot 'butter'.

# ROAST CHICKEN WITH PRESERVED LEMON STUFFING

*serves 4*

The zingy and warm flavours of preserved lemon and ginger permeate this chicken and its couscous stuffing. The stuffing becomes a flavoursome side dish.

1 cup couscous
1 tablespoon olive oil
3 tablespoons slivered almonds, toasted
¼ preserved lemon, skin only, finely sliced
2 cm piece of ginger, peeled and grated
sea salt
freshly ground black pepper

1 tablespoon sweet paprika
1 teaspoon ground cinnamon
1 teaspoon ground cumin
1 teaspoon ground coriander
2 onions, sliced into thick rounds
1.6 kg free-range chicken
250 ml white wine

To make the stuffing, put the couscous and oil in a medium bowl. Pour over 250 ml of boiling water and cover with plastic wrap. Allow to stand for 10 minutes, then uncover and fluff up the couscous with a fork. Stir through the almonds, preserved lemon and ginger and season with salt and pepper. Set aside.

Combine the spices in a small bowl and mix well.

Preheat the oven to 220°C. Lay the onion slices in 2 rows down the centre of a roasting tray with them just touching one another. Rinse and pat the chicken dry and place it on top of the onions. Dust the top of the chicken with the spice mix and season with salt and pepper. Stuff the chicken with the couscous, then tie its legs together. Pour the wine into the tray and place the tray in the oven. Roast for 15 minutes, then baste the chicken with the tray juices and turn the oven down to 180°C. Continue to cook the chicken for a further 45–60 minutes, or until cooked through. Cut the chicken into pieces and serve with the couscous stuffing.

# FOOLPROOF CHICKEN

*serves 6*

This is one dish you can be confident with regardless of your culinary skills. It's great to serve at dinner parties as the chicken is extremely succulent and definitely a crowd pleaser. The succulence of the meat comes from it being steeped in a liquidy marinade that verges on a brine. Serve it with Green-envy Vegetables (page 32).

125 ml apple-cider vinegar

80 ml honey

1 lemon, zested, and juiced to give
2 tablespoons juice

1 lime, zested, and juiced to give
1 tablespoon juice

3 garlic cloves, crushed

12 sage leaves, roughly chopped

1 tablespoon thyme leaves

1 tablespoon sea salt

1 litre water

6 x 200 g free-range chicken breasts,
skin on

Combine the ingredients other than the chicken in a large bowl. Add the chicken breasts – they should be covered in the liquid. Cover and refrigerate for 2-3 hours.

Preheat the oven to 180°C. Remove the chicken breasts from the liquid and place in a baking dish. Cover with a lid or foil and bake for 30-35 minutes until cooked through.

# knowing how food affects us

I don't believe in totally excluding foods from your diet, or that anything is completely good or bad for you. When it comes to what we eat, nothing is black and white. However, there are some foods we should be steered towards, and others we should only eat in moderation. White rice, for example, is really not good enough for you to justify the amount that people eat. In regards to its GI, most white rice is actually higher than sugar. It's not that rice is ultimately bad for you and should be avoided at all times – but not eating it all the time is the key, and eating smaller portions. And generally knowing how what you consume affects your body.

# CHICKEN TENDERLOIN SKEWERS

serves 6

Asian flavours work incredibly well with chicken, and then when you add the flame-grill taste of the barbecue – it rocks. These skewers are flavoured with coriander root, and are a perfect follow-up to Cool Thai Curry Soup (page 52).

4 teaspoons black peppercorns
12 coriander roots, cleaned and roughly chopped
2 garlic cloves
6 tablespoons peanut oil
2 tablespoon ground turmeric
4 teaspoons sea salt
2 teaspoons sugar
1 kg free-range chicken tenderloins, trimmed of fat
lemon

Put the peppercorns in a mortar and grind to a powder. Add the coriander root and garlic and crush finely. Stir in the oil, turmeric, salt and sugar.

Put the tenderloins in a bowl and cover with the marinade, mixing well. Refrigerate for 1 hour, or overnight if possible.

Soak some bamboo skewers (enough for 1 per tenderloin) in water for 30 minutes.

Thread the tenderloins onto the skewers. Heat a large frying pan or barbecue grill over medium heat. Cook the tenderloins for 3–4 minutes on each side, until cooked through. Serve with a squeeze of lemon juice.

I AM A BIG FAN OF CORIANDER ROOT. WHEN I BUY BUNCHES OF CORIANDER, I ALWAYS CUT THE ROOTS STRAIGHT OFF, CLEAN THEM (I USE A STAINLESS-STEEL SCOURER) AND PUT THEM IN A BAG IN THE FREEZER. THERE ARE SO MANY RECIPES THAT BENEFIT FROM THEIR SUBTLE FLAVOUR – MILDER THAN CORIANDER LEAVES. THEY WORK PARTICULARLY WELL IN MARINADES.

# GREEN CHICKEN CURRY

*serves 4*

This is my version of a traditional Thai green curry, a dish that everyone seems to love. In terms of flavour, it's all about the homemade curry paste, with the addition of a few extra kaffir lime leaves. I like to serve the curry with steamed green beans.

2 tablespoons vegetable oil

3 tablespoons Green Curry Paste (page 19)

4 kaffir lime leaves, finely shredded

1 small green chilli, sliced

750 ml coconut milk

1 tablespoon fish sauce

1 teaspoon sugar

600 g free-range chicken breasts, sliced

1 small tin of bamboo shoots, rinsed

1 zucchini, finely sliced on an angle

200 g snow peas, strings removed, cut in half

250 g button mushrooms, sliced

mint, Thai basil (or regular basil) and coriander leaves to garnish

Heat the oil in a wok over medium heat and add the curry paste, lime leaves and chilli. Fry for 2–3 minutes, until fragrant. Add the coconut milk, fish sauce and sugar and bring to the boil.

Add the chicken and bamboo shoots and cook for 25–30 minutes, until the sauce has thickened. Add the zucchini, snow peas and mushrooms and continue to cook for 5 minutes, until the vegetables are tender. Remove from the heat and garnish with the herbs.

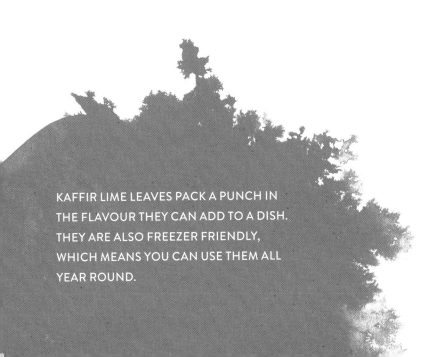

KAFFIR LIME LEAVES PACK A PUNCH IN THE FLAVOUR THEY CAN ADD TO A DISH. THEY ARE ALSO FREEZER FRIENDLY, WHICH MEANS YOU CAN USE THEM ALL YEAR ROUND.

# CHICKEN LARB SAN CHOI BAO

serves 4 (or 12 as a starter)

This may be the first recipe you should make from this cookbook, as it is so easy. It is the kind of dish that after making it once, you can take ownership of and begin adding a little more of this or that.

Larb is actually a minced-meat dish from northern Thailand, while san choi bao is the classic Chinese preparation of flavoursome mince served in lettuce cups – I think you will agree that the two work very well combined! For a quick meal on your own, you can skip making the lettuce cups and shred it instead and chow down.

2 iceberg lettuces, soaked in water
  for 30 minutes
1 tablespoon peanut oil
500 g minced free-range chicken
freshly ground white pepper
2 tablespoons fish sauce
1 tablespoon soy sauce
2 teaspoons sesame oil
3 spring onions, finely sliced
1 kaffir lime leaf, finely shredded

2 lemongrass stalks (white part only), finely
  chopped
1 long red chilli, finely sliced
1 cup coriander leaves
1 cup mint leaves, roughly chopped
2 tablespoons Nahm Jim (page 22)
80 ml lime juice
sea salt
3 tablespoons cashews, roasted and roughly
  chopped

Drain the lettuces and bang them, core-side down, on a bench to help loosen the cores, then use your hands to twist the cores out. Gently peel off the leaves one by one and use scissors to trim around the leaves to form neat cups. Reserve the trimmings and any broken leaves for a salad.

Heat the oil in a wok over medium heat. Add the minced chicken and fry for 4–5 minutes, breaking up any large lumps with a wooden spoon. Season with white pepper. Add the fish sauce, soy sauce, sesame oil, spring onion and kaffir lime leaf and continue to cook for another 2–3 minutes.

Remove the wok from the heat and stir in the lemongrass, chilli, herbs, nahm jim and lime juice. Add salt to taste.

Serve in the lettuce cups garnished with the cashews.

# EUCALYPTUS-INFUSED TURKEY

*serves 4*

This dish came about when I was in the kitchen staring out the window and wondering what to cook for dinner. A eucalyptus tree caught my eye and I thought about how I could use eucalyptus in my cooking.

Eucalyptus leaves give flavour and aroma to the succulent turkey tenderloins, and there's an extra flavour boost from kaffir lime leaves. It's a great dish to serve for Australia Day if you're that way inclined. I like to serve it with Quinoa with Silverbeet (page 37) or a simple green salad with a mustard vinaigrette.

3 tablespoons sugar
500 ml water
50 young eucalyptus leaves
1 cup macadamias, roasted and chopped
4 x 180 g turkey tenderloins
16 kaffir lime leaves

Put the sugar and water in a medium saucepan and bring to the boil. Reduce the heat, add the eucalyptus leaves and simmer for 1 hour, or until reduced and syrupy. Strain the liquid, discarding the leaves, and leave to cool to room temperature. Stir through the macadamias.

Preheat the oven to 180°C. Lay out four 20 cm squares of foil on a work surface. Place a turkey tenderloin in the middle of each square and bend and fold the foil up around the turkey to form a 'boat'. Spoon the eucalyptus and macadamia sauce over the tenderloins, giving each an even crust of macadamias.

Use a small, sharp knife to cut 4 slits in each kaffir lime leaf, keeping them intact. Place 4 leaves on top of each tenderloin. Transfer the foil packages (open at the top) to an oven tray and bake for 25–30 minutes, or until the turkey is cooked through.

EVERYONE KNOWS SOMEONE WITH A CITRUS TREE. CITRUS IS A GREAT FLAVOUR ENHANCER. I USE CITRUS JUICE IN A LOT OF MY RECIPES, BUT ALSO PLENTY OF GRATED ZEST. BE CAREFUL TO USE JUST THE VERY OUTSIDE OF THE RIND AS THE WHITE PITH CAN BE VERY BITTER. I RECOMMEND USING A SUPER-FINE GRATER SUCH AS A MICROPLANE.

When talking about red meat, it's important to mention cuts, portion sizes and how regularly you should eat it. Lean cuts are what we should go for – as they are highest in protein and obviously lowest in fat – while big servings of fatty or processed meats such as sausages should be avoided. Red meat is an excellent source of iron, zinc and B vitamins, and lean red meat has been found to have no negative effects on cholesterol and can even be part of a cholesterol-lowering diet.

For portion sizes, yours is probably a lot less than what you think it is, or what restaurants might lead you to think it is. Use the palm of your hand as an indicator of how much you should be eating – it varies for each person. If I'm having steak, I would much rather it be smaller and high quality than massive and average.

I eat red meat including beef, kangaroo, lamb or pork around twice a week. Eating beef less often is definitely a more sustainable option because of the environmental issues with cattle, including the emissions of greenhouse gases such as methane. Where possible, I go for organic grass-fed beef rather than mass-produced grain-fed beef. The reason is that grass-fed cows live a more natural life grazing in paddocks, but also that their meat has a good balance of Omega-3 to Omega-6 fatty acids (1:3 versus around 1:20 in grain-fed meat). While grain-fed meat can sometimes have a softer texture, grass-fed beef wins in flavour. Organic grass-fed beef is pricier than mass-produced beef, but with meat I think we should buy the best quality we can afford and remember not to buy or consume too much of it. Protein should be part of your meal, not all of it, and small portions of high-quality lean meat consumed less often is the way to go for a healthy, balanced and more sustainable diet.

I love kangaroo as another red-meat option in the kitchen, as it is incredibly lean and just as versatile as beef. Its flavour is similar to venison. The idea of eating kangaroo can be quite foreign to many Australians even though it is one of our native animals, but it can be cooked in the same familiar ways, such as roasting or grilling. I give a recipe for marinated fillets served with a sauce spiked with chilli, coffee and dark chocolate. The dish was inspired when I was travelling in Europe and had venison paired with chocolate, which was amazing. I added the chilli – as the combination of chocolate and chilli is another one I love – and the coffee adds a lovely layer of smokiness that reminds me of eating kangaroo cooked on the fire in the Australian bush.

# BEEF

# &

# KANG

# AROO

# MIDDLE EASTERN-INSPIRED
# BEEF TARTARE

*serves 8*

500 g beef fillet
1 egg yolk
1 tablespoon Tabasco sauce
2 small white onions, finely chopped
2 anchovy fillets, finely chopped
1 long green chilli, seeded and finely chopped
¼ cup mint leaves, finely chopped

¼ cup flat-leaf parsley leaves, finely chopped
1 tablespoon capers, rinsed and chopped
1 teaspoon ground cumin
sea salt
freshly ground black pepper
1 tablespoon olive oil

Use a cook's knife and a chopping board to chop the beef very finely – close to the texture of minced meat. Set aside.

Whisk the egg yolk and Tabasco in a large bowl. Mix in half the onion and all of the anchovies, chilli, herbs, capers and cumin. Season with salt and pepper.

Add the beef and oil and use your hands to mix very well. Press the mixture into egg rings set onto plates, then remove the rings and scatter the meat with the remaining onion.

AS WELL AS SPICING THINGS UP, CHILLI CAN CHANGE HOW THE FLAVOUR OF A DISH IS DELIVERED, MAKING YOU NOTICE DIFFERENT ELEMENTS ON YOUR PALATE. CHILLIES ALSO GIVE YOUR METABOLISM A GOOD KICK, MAKING YOU BURN ENERGY FASTER. THEY ARE EXCELLENT TO EAT BEFORE BED AS THEY RAISE YOUR BODY TEMPERATURE, HELPING YOU TO SLEEP AS YOU COOL DOWN.

INCLUDING LENTILS IN THESE BURGERS ADDS AN EXTRA PROTEIN KICK – AND THEY ARE USED IN PLACE OF BREADCRUMBS, SO THEY LOWER THE CARBOHYDRATE CONTENT. HALF THE LENTILS ARE COOKED IN STOCK, WHILE THE OTHER HALF ARE GROUND RAW.

# SPICY BEEF AND LENTIL BURGERS

*serves 6–8*

I serve these burgers in lettuce leaves rather than hamburger buns, as it allows you to enjoy a burger meal but feel good after it. I add caramelised onion, tomato sauce and Japanese mayonnaise, but you can use any of your favourite accompaniments – sauces, pickles, beetroot, mustard; the list goes on.

1 cup brown lentils
1 litre Rich Beef or Veal Stock (page 16)
1 tablespoon olive oil
2 onions, finely chopped
2 garlic cloves, crushed
500 g lean minced beef
3 eggs, lightly beaten
1 tablespoon grated lemon zest
2 tablespoons Harissa (page 20)
sea salt
freshly ground black pepper

**TO SERVE**
3 red onions, finely sliced
iceberg lettuce leaves
Tomato Sauce (page 23)
Japanese mayonnaise

Place half the lentils and all of the stock in a medium saucepan and bring to the boil. Boil for 15 minutes, then reduce the heat to a simmer and continue to cook uncovered for 30 minutes, or until all the stock has been absorbed by the lentils. Keep an eye on the lentils towards the end to make sure they don't catch on the bottom of the pan. Fluff the lentils up with a fork and leave to cool.

Put the remaining lentils in a food processor and blend to a powder.

Heat the oil in a frying pan over medium heat. Add the onion and fry for 2–3 minutes, until starting to soften. Add the garlic and fry for another 3 minutes, or until the onion is just starting to colour. Leave to cool.

Combine the minced beef, cooked lentils, lentil powder, fried onion, egg, lemon zest and harissa in a large bowl. Season with salt and pepper and mix well. Form into 10 cm burgers. Refrigerate until needed.

To make caramelised onions for the burgers, put the red onion in a heavy-based saucepan with 3 tablespoons of water. Bring to the boil. Cover with a lid, reduce the heat to a simmer and cook for 10–12 minutes until very tender and starting to caramelise.

Heat a non-stick frying pan or barbecue grill over high heat and cook the burgers for 3–4 minutes on each side, or until cooked to your liking.

Serve the burgers in lettuce leaves topped with the caramelised onions, tomato sauce and mayonnaise.

# find the exercise you like

I am not someone that naturally stays in shape – I have to work at it.

An important thing about exercising is finding the kind you enjoy. I like to vary my exercise. As soon as I get sick of doing one thing, I give it a break and move on to something else – the main thing is that whatever you do, not to overdo it, so you still want to do it again. And I think you should always have one day off a week.

# MRS COWLEY'S BRONTOSAURUS BEEF

*serves 6*

This recipe is a special treat, flouting the guidelines about how much meat we should eat. Sometimes it's important to indulge! To even out the over-the-top masculinity of the barbecued meat, serve it with some extra-healthy sides, such as Cauliflower Couscous (page 46) and a green salad.

Mrs Cowley is the mother of one of my friends and it took me forever to get this recipe out of her. The rib eye is marinated for 24 hours (this also works well with steaks), then the whole piece is grilled slowly on the barbecue before being rested and carved into individual ribs. This is Fred Flintstone-style cooking at its best! If you have access to a bay tree, you might like to use a bay leaf twig and pierce the rib eye all the way through the middle of the meat before grilling, to add extra flavour.

250 ml lemon juice
125 ml soy sauce
3 tablespoons brown sugar
3 tablespoons vegetable oil
6 cm piece of ginger, peeled and grated
4 garlic cloves, crushed
standing rib roast of beef with 6 ribs, trimmed of fat

Combine the lemon juice, soy sauce, sugar, oil, ginger and garlic in a bowl and stir until the sugar dissolves. Place the beef in a large dish or container and pour over the marinade, coating well. Cover and refrigerate for 24 hours.

Preheat a barbecue grill to medium-high. Sear the beef for 3 minutes on each side until browned. Reduce the heat to medium, cover the beef with foil or the hood of the barbecue and continue to cook for 50-55 minutes for medium-rare. Leave to rest for 15 minutes before slicing between each rib and serving.

HOW TO BOOST FLAVOUR WITHOUT FAT? MARINATING IS THE ANSWER. WHEN YOU MARINATE MEAT, YOU GET A BIG BOOST OF FLAVOUR WITHOUT FAT, WHILE ALSO HELPING TO RETAIN MOISTURE WITHIN THE MEAT DURING COOKING. IT'S PARTICULARLY USEFUL WHEN USING LEAN CUTS OF MEAT.

# BEEF WITH TZATZIKI

serves 4–6

This is a variation of the common combination of lamb and tzatziki. It works very well for beef fillet cooked on the barbecue, making this an excellent dish for summer. It is great served with Lentils du Puy (page 31).

## TZATZIKI
250 ml Greek-style yoghurt
1 long cucumber, finely chopped
1 garlic clove, crushed
2 tablespoons chopped mint
1 tablespoon lemon juice

800 g beef fillet
1 teaspoon ground cumin
sea salt
freshly ground black pepper

Combine the ingredients for the tzatziki in a bowl and mix well.

Preheat a barbecue grill to medium-high. Sprinkle the beef fillet with the cumin and season well with salt and pepper. Rub the seasoning in with your hands. Cook the fillet for 5–6 minutes on all sides. Rest for 10 minutes, then slice thickly and serve with the tzatziki.

WE ALL KNOW THAT YOGHURT WORKS WONDERS FOR COOLING DOWN YOUR MOUTH AFTER A SPICY DISH. LIKE MILK, IT IS A GOOD SOURCE OF CALCIUM, PHOSPHORUS, PROTEIN, RIBOFLAVIN AND VITAMIN B12, BUT THE FRIENDLY BACTERIA IT CONTAINS ARE ALSO REALLY GOOD FOR YOUR STOMACH, HELPING TO DIGEST FOOD, PREVENT STOMACH INFECTIONS AND ENCOURAGE MORE FRIENDLY BACTERIA TO PROLIFERATE.

# BEEF SILVERSIDE IN RAGU SAUCE

*serves 6-8*

I find that traditional roast beef can lack flavour and be a bit dry. This is what I prefer to cook – a joint of beef stewed in a light Italian-style tomato sauce with stock and red wine, and plenty of vegetables. The beef is sliced as you would a roast and served with the sauce and vegetables – no pasta required. Parsnip Mash (page 30) or White-bean Puree (page 30) are good side dishes.

2 tablespoons olive oil

1 tablespoon butter

1.5 kg fresh beef silverside, trimmed of fat

3 leeks, finely chopped

2 onions, finely chopped

2 garlic cloves, crushed

2 carrots, finely chopped

2 celery stalks, finely chopped

1 red capsicum, finely chopped

pinch of sweet paprika

1 tablespoon tomato paste

250 ml red wine

375 ml Rich Beef or Veal Stock (page 16)

sea salt

freshly ground black pepper

185 ml tomato puree

10 basil leaves, torn

1 tablespoon oregano leaves

1 tablespoon cream

2 tablespoons chopped flat-leaf parsley

Heat the oil and butter in a large heavy-based saucepan over medium heat. Add the piece of silverside and fry for 2-3 minutes on each side, until well browned all over. Add the leek, onion, garlic, carrot, celery, capsicum, paprika, tomato paste, wine and stock, and season with salt and pepper. Bring to the boil and cook for 5-6 minutes, then reduce the heat to a simmer, cover with a lid and cook for 30 minutes.

Add the tomato puree, basil and oregano, cover again with the lid and cook for another hour, or until the beef is very tender.

Remove the beef from the sauce and allow to rest for 10 minutes before slicing thickly. Meanwhile, taste and adjust the seasoning of the sauce and stir in the cream and parsley. Serve the sliced beef with the sauce and vegetables.

BEEF SILVERSIDE IS ONE OF MY FAVOURITE MEATS TO COOK WITH AS IT'S INEXPENSIVE BUT GOOD QUALITY, AND LEAN. IT BECOMES MELTINGLY TENDER WHEN COOKED IN A SAUCE LIKE THIS.

# VEAL WITH CAPER
# AND RED ONION GREMOLATA

*serves 4*

This is rustic fast food. You can pick up the ingredients on your way home from work, then chop and toss them together, and throw the veal in the pan. Just be careful not to overcook the veal as it will become tough.

2 tablespoons capers, rinsed and chopped
1 red onion, finely chopped
1 anchovy fillet, finely chopped
3 tablespoons chopped flat-leaf parsley
grated zest of 1 lemon
freshly ground black pepper
4 x 180 g veal scaloppine
sea salt

### ROCKET AND PARMESAN SALAD

3 tablespoons olive oil
2 tablespoons lemon juice
250 g rocket
50 g parmesan, shaved

Combine the capers, onion, anchovy, parsley and lemon zest in a small bowl and season with pepper. Set aside.

To make the salad, combine the oil and lemon juice in a medium bowl. Add the rocket and parmesan and toss well.

Season the veal slices with salt and pepper. Heat a large frying pan or barbecue grill over high heat. Cook the veal slices for 1–2 minutes on each side.

Scatter the veal with the caper and red onion gremolata and serve with the salad.

# CHILLI KANGAROO
# WITH COFFEE AND CHOCOLATE SAUCE

*serves 6*

If people can get their head around having chocolate and chilli together, then having chocolate with meat – and a splash of coffee too – shouldn't be too much of a stretch. You might be surprised at how savoury this dish tastes. Chocolate doesn't always have to be associated with sweetness, and Mexicans have been eating unsweetened chocolate for centuries.

This dish is great served with wilted baby spinach or Roasted Pumpkin and Hazelnut Salad (page 45).

2 tablespoons olive oil
2 small red chillies, finely chopped
sea salt
freshly ground black pepper
6 x 180 g kangaroo fillets (or beef)
185 ml Rich Beef or Veal Stock (page 16)

80 ml red wine
1 garlic clove, bruised
sprig of rosemary
3 tablespoons freshly brewed espresso coffee
30 g dark chocolate with 70% cocoa solids, grated

Combine the oil and chilli in a medium bowl and season with salt and pepper. Add the kangaroo fillets and coat well. Marinate in the refrigerator for 2 hours (or longer if you like your food spicy).

Combine the stock, wine, garlic and rosemary in a small saucepan and place over high heat. Boil for 8-10 minutes, until the liquid reduces by half. Remove the garlic and rosemary from the pan and add the coffee. Simmer for another 5-6 minutes (don't boil rapidly as the coffee may become bitter). Remove from the heat and add the chocolate, stirring until melted.

Heat a frying pan over medium-high heat and cook the kangaroo fillets for 2-3 minutes on each side, for medium-rare. Allow to rest for 10 minutes. Slice the kangaroo thickly and serve with the coffee and chocolate sauce.

KANGAROO IS A GREAT RED MEAT TO INCORPORATE INTO YOUR DIET, IT'S SUPER LEAN AND GOOD FOR THE ENVIRONMENT AS KANGAROOS DON'T PRODUCE ANY METHANE TO POLLUTE THE ATMOSPHERE. WHEN COOKING KANGAROO, AIM TO COOK IT MEDIUM-RARE. EVEN WHEN SLIGHTLY OVERCOOKED, THE MEAT CAN BECOME VERY TOUGH.

I've always loved lamb. I'm a big fan of it and would say it is my favourite meat overall. This probably gives away my Australianness straight away, as we eat plenty of lamb in Australia compared to countries such as the United States.

As with other meats, lamb is an excellent source of protein, iron, zinc, B vitamins and selenium – in fact, it has slightly more iron than beef. The cut of lamb that I like best is the shoulder, even though it does tend to have more fat on it than the typical leg of lamb. I trim off all the excess fat and accept the marbled fat. Lamb shoulder is perfect in slow-cooked dishes such as stews.

I really urge you to try two dishes in this chapter – the *Seven-hour Lamb* and the *Yoghurt Soup with Minted Meatballs*.

If you want to impress dinner guests, then the pot-roasted Seven-hour Lamb is the one. You can literally serve it with a spoon – the lamb is so tender it just falls apart.

The Yoghurt Soup with Minted Meatballs is a twist on the classic combination of lamb, yoghurt and mint, which go together like tomatoes and basil. Usually, of course, the lamb is the focus and the yoghurt and mint are flavours or accompaniments, but here the smooth yoghurt soup is the base and the lamb meatballs are the accent. Home cooking is all about experimentation and learning along the way – you can take a successful flavour combination like this one and turn it on its head.

# LAMB STEW WITH GREMOLATA

*serves 6*

This is a simple Italian-inspired dish. The classic ingredients of onion, carrot, celery, leek, tomato, garlic, herbs and red wine all cook to a thick stew studded with pieces of lamb. The stew is thickened with a grated potato. It is all lightened and livened up with the addition of zesty gremolata, and is perfect with Parsnip Mash (page 30) or White-bean Puree (page 30).

2 tablespoons olive oil

800 g lamb shoulder or leg meat, trimmed of fat and cut into 3 cm cubes

3 onions, chopped

3 carrots, chopped

3 celery stalks, sliced

1 leek, sliced

800 g vine-ripened tomatoes, peeled and roughly chopped

4 garlic cloves, finely chopped

4 sage leaves, finely chopped

sprig of rosemary

750 ml water

125 ml red wine

1 potato, peeled and grated

Gremolata (page 22)

Heat half a tablespoon of the oil in a heavy-based saucepan over medium-high heat. Add half the lamb and cook for 2–3 minutes, until the meat is browned all over. Remove to a plate, then brown the remaining lamb in another half a tablespoon of oil, and remove to the plate.

Reduce the heat of the pan to medium and add the remaining oil. Fry the onion, carrot, celery and leek for 4–5 minutes, until just softening. Return the lamb to the pan with the tomato, garlic, sage, rosemary, water and wine and bring to the boil. Add the potato, reduce the heat to a simmer, cover and cook for 1½ hours, or until the lamb is tender and the sauce is thick.

Scatter with gremolata and serve.

# SEVEN-HOUR LAMB

## serves 6–8

This French dish may take seven hours to cook, but it only takes twenty minutes of preparation, and the meat becomes so soft you can serve it with a spoon. The lamb is pot-roasted, and the pot is sealed with dough to make sure all the juices stay in. You put the pot in the oven at, say, 11 am in the morning, then enjoy the aromas from the oven all day.

I like to break the dough seal at the table when everyone is seated, and I think Parsnip Mash (page 30) and sautéed button mushrooms tossed in a little oil and thyme make great accompaniments. This is a great dish for winter entertaining.

150 g pancetta
20 garlic cloves
1 tablespoon rosemary leaves
1 tablespoon olive oil
2 kg leg of lamb
sea salt
freshly ground black pepper
4 carrots, cut into 3 cm chunks
2 bunches swollen spring onions
  (white part only), trimmed

2 leeks, finely sliced
1 bouquet garni made of 1 bay leaf,
  4 parsley stalks and 2 thyme sprigs
  tied with string
250 ml white wine
150 g (1 cup) plain flour
185 ml water

Preheat the oven to 125°C. Roughly chop the pancetta, then add 4 of the garlic cloves and the rosemary and chop together until fine.

Pour the olive oil onto the leg of lamb and season well with salt and pepper. Massage the oil, salt and pepper in with your hands.

Use a small, sharp knife to cut 16 small incisions across the surface of the leg of lamb. Stuff a teaspoon of the pancetta mixture into each incision.

Put the lamb, remaining garlic cloves, carrot, spring onions, leek, bouquet garni and wine in a heavy ovenproof pot or casserole dish and cover with a tight-fitting lid. Place the pot on top of an oven tray.

Mix the flour and water in a small mixing bowl and use your hands to press the dough around the join of the pot and lid. The dough will set in the oven and ensure the pot is well sealed. The tray should catch any drips of dough.

Bake for 7 hours, then break the seal at the table and serve the lamb and vegetables with a spoon.

# drinking alcohol

I use wine and spirits as flavourings in my cooking, knowing that most of the
alcohol they contain burns off when I cook them. Drinking alcohol is something
I consider a little more carefully, however. I think that if you want to have a glass
of wine with dinner, you might have to rule out dessert, as both are very high in
sugar and should be seen as treats, not everyday meal accompaniments.

# LAMB STEAKS
# WITH HERBS AND HARISSA

serves 6

This dish is extremely quick and easy – all the preparation lies in the marinade.
I honestly don't know what I would do without harissa, as it makes everything taste
fantastic. I like to serve these steaks with a rocket salad.

¼ cup mint leaves, finely chopped
¼ cup coriander leaves, finely chopped
2 tablespoons Harissa (page 20)
1 tablespoon olive oil
1 tablespoon lemon juice
1 tablespoon tomato paste
1 tablespoon ground cumin
1 teaspoon ground coriander
1 teaspoon ground turmeric
6 lamb-leg steaks (about 700 g)

Combine the ingredients other than the lamb in a medium bowl and mix well. Add the lamb and
coat thoroughly. Marinate in the refrigerator for 4 hours.

Heat a barbecue grill to medium. Wipe the excess marinade from the steaks and cook for 4
minutes on each side, or until cooked to your liking.

# ZUCCHINI AND CAPSICUM
# WITH SPICED LAMB STUFFING

*serves 4–6*

This is a great way to introduce fussy eaters or people who are anti-vegetables to just how good vegetables can taste. There is meat to flavour the vegetables, but still a good variety of vegetables in the meal.

500 ml Tomato Sauce (page 23)
6 tomatoes, 4 chopped and 2 sliced
6 medium zucchini
2 red capsicums
1 tablespoon olive oil, plus extra for drizzling
2 red onions, finely chopped
3 garlic cloves, crushed
1 tablespoon ground ginger

1 tablespoon ground cinnamon
1 teaspoon sweet paprika
½ teaspoon ground cumin
½ teaspoon freshly ground black pepper
600 g lean minced lamb
¼ cup flat-leaf parsley leaves, roughly chopped
1 tablespoon dried mint
⅓ cup brown rice, ground (i.e. in a spice grinder)

Put the tomato sauce in a medium saucepan over medium heat and simmer for 10 minutes to thicken a little more. Remove from the heat and stir through the chopped tomato. Pour into a large baking dish.

Cut the zucchini in half lengthwise and use a teaspoon to hollow out the halves, creating some room for the stuffing. Set the scraped-out flesh aside for another recipe. Cut the capsicums in half through the core and remove the seeds. Set the zucchini and capsicum aside.

To make the filling, heat the oil in a heavy-based saucepan over medium heat. Add the onion and fry for 2–3 minutes, until softened. Add the garlic and ground spices and cook, stirring, for 2–3 minutes. The mixture should be fragrant. Add the minced lamb and stir to break up any large lumps, then add the parsley and mint and cook for 10 minutes. Add the ground brown rice and cook for a further 10 minutes, stirring regularly to ensure the mixture doesn't catch on the bottom of the pan.

Preheat the oven to 180°C. Spoon the mince into the capsicum halves. Place on top of the tomato sauce in the baking dish, and cover with the sliced tomatoes.

Spoon more mince into 6 of the zucchini halves, and top with the other halves as lids. Secure the lids to the bases using toothpicks. Put the stuffed zucchini in the dish with the capsicums. Drizzle the vegetables with a little extra oil and cover with foil. Bake in the oven for 45–50 minutes, or until the vegetables are tender.

THE GROUND BROWN RICE IN THIS STUFFING HELPS TO ABSORB LIQUID IN THE SAME WAY THAT BREADCRUMBS WOULD. AS THE VEGETABLES COOK, THEY RELEASE WATER, SO THIS IS A GREAT WAY TO SOAK UP THEIR NUTRIENTS AND FLAVOURS AND REDUCE THE LIQUID IN THE DISH.

LAMB

# RED LAMB BACKSTRAPS
# WITH CHILLI COLESLAW

*serves 4*

With this dish I wanted to reinvent the typical coleslaw that we all know, minus the mayonnaise, and add some Thai influences. It works really well with the lamb marinated in red curry paste. This meal is quick to cook, super healthy and perfect for the barbecue.

3 x 200 g lamb backstraps
2 tablespoons Red Curry Paste (page 19)
1 tablespoon sesame oil

### CHILLI COLESLAW

3 tablespoons lime juice
2 tablespoons Nahm Jim (page 22)
1 tablespoon fish sauce
3 teaspoons grated palm sugar
2 kaffir lime leaves, finely shredded
2 lemongrass stalks (white part only), finely chopped
½ red cabbage (about 300 g), shredded
1 bunch radishes, grated
2 carrots, grated
90 g (1 cup) bean sprouts, trimmed
1 cup coriander leaves
½ cup vietnamese mint leaves, roughly chopped

Marinate the lamb in the curry paste and sesame oil for 2-4 hours.

To make the coleslaw dressing, combine the lime juice, nahm jim, fish sauce, palm sugar, kaffir lime leaves and lemongrass in a small bowl and stir until the sugar dissolves.

Combine the remaining ingredients in a large bowl and pour over the dressing. Mix until well combined.

Preheat a large frying pan or barbecue grill to medium-high. Wipe the excess marinade from the backstraps and cook for 3 minutes on each side, or until cooked to your liking. Rest the backstraps for 10 minutes, then slice thickly and serve with the coleslaw.

# YOGHURT SOUP
# WITH MINTED MEATBALLS

*serves 4*

This is a Turkish dish that I first tried in Tanzania, of all places. I was visiting a school that is funded out of Turkey and was there for Dignity Day. All the children had to define what dignity was to them, and it was incredible to realise what a universal concept it is. I think it is hard to define, but easier if you think of an experience where dignity is taken away.

As for this soup, I really liked it. Everyone has tried lamb with tzatziki, so the dish isn't really that bizarre, just a new way of serving it.

500 g minced lamb
½ cup pine nuts, toasted and roughly chopped
1 onion, finely chopped
1 egg, lightly beaten
2 tablespoons dried mint
2 teaspoons ground cumin
1 tablespoon ground coriander
1 tablespoon grated lemon zest

sea salt
freshly ground black pepper
1 litre Chicken Stock (page 15)
6 garlic cloves, bruised
1 litre natural yoghurt
fresh mint leaves to serve
Harissa (page 20) to serve

Preheat the oven to 200°C and line an oven tray with baking paper.

Combine the minced lamb, pine nuts, onion, egg, dried mint, spices and lemon zest in a large bowl. Season with salt and pepper and mix well. Roll into 24 balls and place on the prepared tray. Bake in the oven for 10-12 minutes, or until well browned.

Combine the stock and garlic in a saucepan and bring to the boil, then reduce the heat and simmer for 8-10 minutes. Allow to cool slightly, then pour into a food processor along with the yoghurt and blend until smooth.

Spoon the warm soup into 4 bowls and add 6 meatballs to each. Garnish with mint leaves and dollops of harissa.

IT IS IMPORTANT TO HAVE GOOD HOMEMADE STOCK FOR THIS SOUP, AS WELL AS SOME TASTY HARISSA, AS THEY BOTH MAKE A BIG DIFFERENCE TO THE FINISHED DISH.

# cooking to have leftovers

It's great to be prepared for times when you're too tired or too busy to make a meal. During times when you cook a lot, divide your leftovers into individual portions and throw them in the freezer. Leftovers can also inspire new dishes.

You can also be a bit more systematic about it and cook extra food on purpose, such as making a big quantity on Sunday when you know you've got a busy week coming up. Sunday is usually my cooking day. I make a lot of mess but set myself up for the week, it's so much better than resorting to take-away.

# MOROCCAN LAMB IN TOMATO JAM

*serves 4*

In this dish the stove really does all the work, gently cooking the tomatoes down to an amazing thick, rich sauce, and rendering the pieces of lamb beautifully tender. The dish is scattered with almonds fried in just a little butter. I like to serve it with vegetables or a green salad and a little couscous, or with Quinoa with Silverbeet (page 37).

1.5 kg tomatoes
1–2 tablespoons olive oil
1.5 kg trimmed lamb shoulder or leg meat, cut into 3 cm cubes
3 onions, finely chopped
3 garlic cloves, crushed
2 teaspoons ground ginger
1 cinnamon stick

pinch of saffron threads
1 teaspoon freshly ground black pepper
sea salt
1 tablespoon butter
⅓ cup blanched almonds
1½ tablespoons honey
1 teaspoon ground cinnamon

Cut the tomatoes in half and squeeze them over a bowl to remove the seeds. Discard the seeds and finely chop the flesh. Set aside.

Heat a little oil in a large heavy-based saucepan over medium–high heat and fry one-third of the lamb for 2–3 minutes, until browned all over. Remove to a plate and continue to brown the remaining lamb in two more batches with a little extra oil each time. Remove all the lamb to the plate.

Reduce the heat of the pan to medium and add the onion. Fry for 2–3 minutes, until starting to soften. Add the garlic, ground ginger, cinnamon stick, saffron and pepper and cook for a further 2 minutes. Return the lamb to the pan along with the tomatoes and season with salt. Cover with a lid and simmer for 2 hours, stirring occasionally.

Remove the lid and cook for a final 15–20 minutes uncovered, or until the sauce is very thick. Meanwhile, melt the butter in a small frying pan over medium heat. Add the almonds and fry for 2–3 minutes, stirring, until golden brown.

Remove the cinnamon stick from the lamb, and stir in the honey and ground cinnamon. Serve scattered with the fried almonds.

IN THIS DISH I USE BOTH A CINNAMON STICK AND GROUND CINNAMON – THE STICK IS ADDED AT THE BEGINNING TO IMPART ITS SUBTLE FLAVOURS, WHILE THE GROUND CINNAMON IS STIRRED IN AT THE END TO ADD A MORE PROMINENT CINNAMON TASTE.

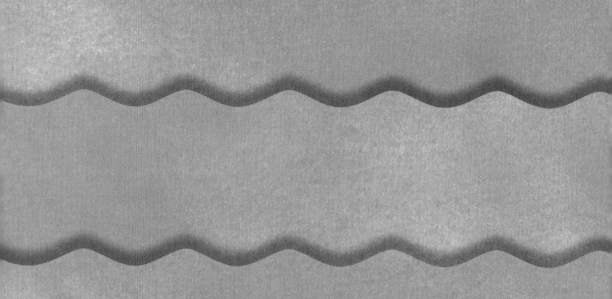

I've only recently rediscovered pork after an unfortunate pork crackling experience when I was younger. One Christmas, I completely over-indulged on crackling to the point where I made myself sick. It took me years to be able to stomach pork again.

I now know that pork is a delicious and lean meat – some cuts are just as lean as skinless chicken breasts – that is very versatile. All meats are an excellent source of protein, iron, zinc, B vitamins and other nutrients, but pork is particularly rich in the B vitamin thiamin, which helps the body convert carbohydrates to energy, among other functions.

I prefer free-range pork as the pigs are treated far more humanely, and the meat – like grass-fed beef – is more nutritious, but I still skip the crackling, as I'd prefer to avoid the large dose of fat.

One of the interesting things I've learnt during my travels to Japan is that the people of the Okinawa Islands have what is thought to be the highest life expectancy in the world – and they live the healthiest lives. Japan gets high marks in this regard too, but it is thought that one of the factors putting the Okinawans ahead of the rest of the country is their particular diet. They have a nutrient-rich diet very high in vegetables including seaweed, and low in calories, and also featuring tofu, a small amount of fish and – wait for it – pork! Pork is the main meat they consume.

I'll admit that it probably isn't the pork itself that makes the Okinawans live long lives, but rather the fact that everything is in good balance in their diets. It just goes to show that healthy eating can still include the things you love.

# CHESTNUT, CABBAGE AND PANCETTA SOUP

*serves 4*

A lot of people aren't sure what to do with chestnuts, and they are something often associated with dessert. But their natural sweetness works in savoury dishes too, such as this Italian soup to make in autumn or winter. The chestnuts work very well with the salty pancetta.

To cook chestnuts, slit the skins and boil them for 10–15 minutes until tender, then peel them while hot.

1 litre water
sea salt
200 g cabbage, cut into large chunks
2 garlic cloves, peeled
1 tablespoon olive oil
1 onion, finely chopped

75 g pancetta, finely chopped
1 long rosemary sprig
500 g chestnuts, cooked and peeled
 (to yield 250 g)
freshly ground black pepper
185 ml white wine

Pour the water into a saucepan and season with salt. Bring to the boil and add the cabbage and garlic. Cover with a lid and cook for 10 minutes until the cabbage is soft. Strain the cabbage and reserve the cooking water. Discard the garlic and finely chop the cabbage when it is cool enough to handle.

Heat the oil in a large heavy-based saucepan. Add the onion and pancetta and fry for 2 minutes, until lightly browned. Add the rosemary sprig and fry for another 2 minutes. Add the chestnuts and cabbage and season with salt and pepper. Increase the heat to high, pour in the wine and bring to the boil. Add the reserved cooking water and return to the boil, then reduce the heat to a simmer and cook for another 15 minutes. Remove the rosemary and serve.

# PORK CHOPS WITH PEAR
# AND LILLY PILLY COMPOTE

serves 4

Lilly pillies are the purple berries that grow on native Australian lilly pilly trees. They've been eaten for thousands of years by Aboriginal people. I first tried lilly pillies when a friend introduced them to me on a tour of the botanical gardens in Sydney. After sampling the small fruit, I immediately wanted to include them in a recipe. They give this dish something extra – a slightly peppery taste that partners well with the sweetness of pear. A salad is the perfect accompaniment.

If you can't get hold of lilly pillies, you can make the sauce without them, and garnish the dish with warmed red currants instead (I use frozen if fresh are unavailable).

2 tablespoons soy sauce
1 tablespoon olive oil
1 teaspoon fennel seeds, ground
4 x 180 g butterflied pork chops
500 ml white wine
2 pears, peeled and roughly chopped

12 black peppercorns
2 cm piece of ginger, peeled and finely sliced
2 bay leaves
1 cinnamon stick
16 (120 g) lilly pillies

Combine the soy sauce, oil and ground fennel in a shallow dish. Add the pork and coat well, then leave to marinate for 30 minutes.

Pour the wine into a medium saucepan and bring to the boil. Boil for 3 minutes, then add the pear, peppercorns, ginger, bay leaves and cinnamon stick. Reduce the heat to a simmer and cook for 10 minutes. Add the lilly pillies and cook for another 20 minutes until thick. Remove from the heat and scoop out the peppercorns, bay leaves and cinnamon stick (if the peppercorns aren't visible on the surface, you might have to search for them with the spoon).

Heat a barbecue grill to medium-high. Wipe the excess marinade from the pork chops and cook for 4 minutes on each side.

Serve the chops with the warm compote.

# BACON AND PEA SOUP

## serves 6

Some old-fashioned combinations like bacon or ham with split peas really get it right – these two simple flavours taste amazing together. I like to add fresh peas, leek and celeriac to my version of the soup.

3 litres Chicken Stock (page 15)
2 cups split peas, rinsed
400 g bacon bones
75 g piece of pancetta
1 parmesan rind (optional)
1 medium celeriac, peeled and finely chopped

1 bouquet garni made of 1 bay leaf,
4 parsley stalks and 2 thyme sprigs tied with string
4 leeks, finely sliced
200 g fresh or frozen peas
freshly ground black pepper

Place the stock, split peas, bacon bones, pancetta, parmesan rind (if using), celeriac and bouquet garni in a pot and bring to the boil. Reduce the heat to a simmer, cover with a lid and cook for 1½–2 hours. Remove the lid to skim the surface of any foam or impurities every so often.

Remove the bacon bones, pancetta, parmesan and bouquet garni from the soup, and add the leek. Simmer for a further 10 minutes. Remove from the heat and lightly blend with a stick blender. Bring back to a simmer, add the fresh or frozen peas and cook for a further 5 minutes. Season with pepper and serve.

I FIND IT MUCH MORE CONVENIENT TO WATER MY HOME-GROWN HERBS ONCE A DAY THAN RUN UP TO THE SHOPS WHEN I'VE FORGOTTEN SOMETHING IN THE MIDDLE OF MAKING DINNER. YOU DON'T NEED TO HAVE A BIG BACKYARD TO HAVE A GARDEN. IT'S AMAZING WHAT YOU CAN GROW IN LARGE TUBS IF YOU LIVE IN A UNIT OR SOMEWHERE ELSE LACKING OUTDOOR SPACE.

# JAPANESE PORK WITH ONION DRESSING

serves 2

I'm not always a fan of Japanese salad dressings, but this onion one I absolutely love. What's great about it is that you blend the onion in a food processor and strain it, using the juice to marinate the pork, and the solids as the base for the salad dressing. It's really thick and tastes fantastic.

4 medium onions, roughly chopped
500 g pork fillet
sea salt
freshly ground black pepper
2 tablespoons soy sauce
2 tablespoons rice-wine vinegar

3 tablespoons grapeseed oil
2 teaspoons sesame oil
pinch of ground mustard
pinch of sugar
200 g mixed salad leaves
1 fennel bulb, finely sliced

Put the onion in a food processor and blend until smooth. Press through a fine strainer into a bowl, giving onion juice. Reserve the solids in a separate bowl.

Season the pork with salt and pepper and place in a shallow dish. Pour over the onion juice and coat well. Put the dish of pork and the bowl of onion solids in the refrigerator overnight.

Mix the soy sauce, vinegar, 2 tablespoons of the grapeseed oil, the sesame oil, mustard, sugar and 1 teaspoon of salt into the onion solids. This will be the dressing for the salad.

Heat the remaining grapeseed oil in a large frying pan over medium heat and cook the marinated pork fillet for 7 minutes on each side. Leave to rest for 10 minutes.

Combine the salad leaves, fennel and salad dressing in a bowl and toss well.

Slice the pork thickly and serve with the salad.

# PORK AND BEAN SOUP
# WITH TURNIP PUREE

serves 8

Pork combines with celeriac, carrot, parsnip and cannellini beans in this winter soup, which is topped with dollops of turnip puree. You get a great source of protein from the pork and the beans in the soup; adding beans is a great way to limit your meat consumption.

400 g dried cannellini beans, soaked overnight
olive oil
750 g pork neck, cut into 2 cm cubes
1 tablespoon ground cumin
sea salt
freshly ground black pepper
1.5 litres Chicken Stock (page 15)
250 ml dry white wine
1 medium celeriac, peeled and chopped
4 carrots, peeled and chopped
2 parsnips, peeled and chopped
8 garlic cloves, crushed
1–2 large strips of orange rind
250 ml freshly squeezed orange juice

TURNIP PUREE
500 ml Vegetable Stock (page 17)
1 turnip, peeled and roughly chopped
sea salt
freshly ground white pepper
chopped flat-leaf parsley

Drain and rinse the cannellini beans, then boil them in plenty of water with a splash of olive oil until soft. Drain.

Meanwhile, place the pork in a large bowl and toss with 1 tablespoon of olive oil, the cumin and some salt and black pepper. Heat a large heavy-based saucepan over medium–high heat and cook the pork in batches for 2–3 minutes until the meat is browned all over. Remove to a plate.

Add the chicken stock and wine to the pan and bring to the boil, then reduce the heat to a simmer. Return the pork to the pan along with the celeriac, carrot, parsnip, garlic and orange rind and simmer for 25–30 minutes, or until the vegetables are tender.

Add the beans and orange juice to the pan and cook for another 10 minutes. While the soup is cooking, make the turnip puree. Pour the vegetable stock into a small saucepan and bring to the boil. Add the turnip and cook for 6–8 minutes, or until tender. Transfer to a food processor (or use a stick blender) and blend until smooth. Season with salt and white pepper.

Serve the soup with dollops of the turnip puree and parsley.

# avoiding takeaway

Try not to allow yourself excuses like 'It's just easy' or 'I'm tired' to indulge in pizza or takeaway. If you really feel like pizza, then get it, but make sure it's an occasional treat that you're actually going to enjoy. I think it's helpful to remember that by the time you've ordered pizza and waited for it to come, you could have easily made something simple for yourself.

# PORK NECK TWO WAYS

serves 4

Here are two quick ways for grilled pork neck – each with a different flavoursome marinade. You can choose one recipe or the other. They are both great dinner-party dishes, perhaps served with Vegetable Stir-fry with Miso (page 27) or Broome Vietnamese Salad (page 42).

## PORK WITH FENNEL SEEDS

2 teaspoons fennel seeds
1 teaspoon sea salt
2 x 150 g pieces of pork neck
3 tablespoons hoisin sauce
3 tablespoons soy sauce
2 long cucumbers, sliced thinly

Put the fennel seeds and salt in a mortar and grind until fine. Rub the mixture into the pork and refrigerate for 2 hours.

Preheat a barbecue grill (or oiled frying pan) to medium-high. Combine the hoisin and soy sauces in a small bowl and brush over the pork. Fry the pork for 3-4 minutes on each side. Remove to a plate and rest for 5 minutes before slicing thickly and serving with the cucumber.

## PORK WITH CORIANDER ROOT

6 coriander roots, cleaned and roughly chopped
2 tablespoons black peppercorns
1 tablespoon sugar
3 tablespoons soy sauce
2 tablespoons vegetable oil
2 cm piece of ginger, peeled and cut into chunks
2 x 150 g pieces of pork neck
¼ cup coriander leaves

Put the coriander root, peppercorns and sugar in a mortar and grind until fine. Stir in the soy sauce and oil. Transfer to a shallow dish and add the ginger and pork. Toss to coat the pork well, then marinate in the refrigerator for 2 hours.

Preheat a barbecue grill (or oiled frying pan) to medium-high. Wipe the ginger and excess marinade from the pork and fry for 3-4 minutes on each side. Remove the pork to a plate and rest for 5 minutes. Meanwhile, add the marinade to a saucepan with 3 tablespoons of water and cook for 2-3 minutes, or until reduced by half. Remove the ginger. Slice the pork and serve with the sauce and coriander leaves.

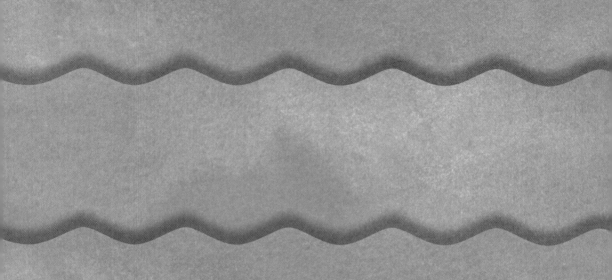

I used to have a big sweet tooth, and still have my favourite desserts, like vanilla pannacotta! However, these days I've trained myself out of the habit of having dessert regularly and usually have it just once a week, such as when I'm entertaining or am out at a restaurant and inspired by something truly delicious on the menu.

Dessert is where a lot of people come undone. You can literally do everything right in your diet, but a plate of dessert can be your downfall – it feels great at the time, but the sugar and fat can undo a whole day's healthy eating. So I try to recognise that wanting dessert is generally a craving rather than hunger, and that once you're in the habit of not looking for something sweet to cap things off, it's quite easy to forget about it.

With dessert being a special treat, I try to make it worthwhile when I do have it! Not in the size of the serving, but in the quality of the dessert. I would rather take the time to prepare and enjoy my Vanilla Pannacotta with Berry Coulis or my Chocolate Soufflé – or eat someone else's delectable and well-made dessert – than binge on copious amounts of something sugary that I ultimately won't find satisfying or will feel bad about later.

A small serve eaten slowly and thoughtfully, so you enjoy every mouthful, is the ideal way of eating dessert. The trick is knowing when enough is enough, even if dessert is on the healthy side. I think it's good to remember that a tub of low-fat ice-cream is still a whole tub of ice-cream!

# DESSERTS

# CHOCOLATE SOUFFLÉ

serves 4

Soufflés are generally lower in fat than most desserts, and always an impressive thing to serve up to your friends. Using chocolate with a high cocoa content means you get a more intense chocolate flavour – and more of the antioxidant benefits of the cacao bean.

icing sugar
200 g dark chocolate with
 70% cocoa solids
3 tablespoons milk
2 egg yolks, lightly beaten
6 egg whites
3 tablespoons caster sugar

Preheat the oven to 180°C. Lightly butter four 250 ml ramekins and dust them with icing sugar. Roll the ramekins around to make sure the sugar completely covers the insides. Place the ramekins on a baking tray.

Put the chocolate and milk in a large heatproof bowl set over a saucepan of simmering water. Stir until the chocolate melts and the mixture is glossy. Remove from the heat and allow to cool slightly, then stir in the egg yolks until well combined. Don't be concerned if the mixture looks curdled.

Beat the egg whites in a clean glass or ceramic bowl until soft peaks form. Begin to add the caster sugar gradually and continue to beat until just before you have firm peaks. Take a large spoonful of the egg whites and beat them into the chocolate with a wooden spoon to loosen the mixture. Then, use a spatula to gently fold the remaining egg whites into the chocolate in three batches.

Spoon the mixture into the prepared ramekins, filling to the top. Use a spatula to wipe across the top of each ramekin to flatten the surface. Run your index finger around the inside lip of the ramekins to create a gap between the soufflé mixture and the ramekin. Bake for 10–12 minutes. The soufflés should be well risen above the ramekins. Serve immediately.

# cooking with a little cream or butter

Yes, cream is high in fat, but I think a small amount spread out among a few people is fairly insignificant for the flavour that it adds. I use a touch of cream or butter when I think
it is really worthwhile in a dish, and with cream, I don't mind if it is regular thickened cream, pure cream or even double cream – just whatever I have in the fridge at the time. Just remember to check the date before adding it (one of my disasters, oops!).

# SEASONAL FRIANDS

*makes 16 friands*

The use of egg whites in friands reduces their fat content, and you can use any fruit you like – peaches, plums, pears, berries and segments of mandarin all work really well. Just visit your local fruit market and check out what's in season.

80 g butter, melted
200 g (2 cups) almond meal
12 egg whites
125 g (1 cup) icing sugar
75 g (½ cup) plain flour
8 peaches, finely sliced (or the equivalent
    of another fruit)

Preheat the oven to 180°C. Butter 16 friand or small muffin holes.

Combine the melted butter, almond meal and egg whites in a large bowl. Sift on the icing sugar and flour and stir until just combined. Spoon into the friand or muffin holes and arrange the peach slices on top. Bake in the oven for 30-35 minutes until a skewer inserted in a friand comes out clean. Leave to cool in the tin for 5 minutes before turning out onto a wire rack.

# MANDARIN CAKE

serves 8

This cake has no flour or sugar — just eggs, almond meal and pureed cooked mandarins. A little sweetness comes with the rosewater syrup that is poured onto the cake.

6 mandarins, whole
4 eggs plus 2 egg whites
300 g (3 cups) almond meal
1 tablespoon baking powder
½ cup chopped unsalted
  pistachios

SYRUP
80 g sugar
1 cinnamon stick
1 star anise
2 cloves
1 cardamom pod, cracked
125 ml water
2 teaspoons rosewater

Put the mandarins in a saucepan, cover with water and weight down with a small plate. Bring to the boil, then reduce the heat and simmer for 45 minutes. Drain and allow to cool slightly, then blend until smooth in a food processor.

Preheat the oven to 180°C. Grease a 22 cm round cake tin and line with baking paper.

Put the mandarin puree, eggs and egg whites, almond meal and baking powder in a large bowl and mix well. Pour into the tin and bake for 40 minutes to 1 hour until a skewer comes out clean.

Meanwhile, combine the syrup ingredients other than the rosewater in a small saucepan and simmer for around 20 minutes, until thickened and syrupy. Remove from the heat and strain out the spices. Add the rosewater.

Pour the hot syrup over the hot cake and leave to cool in the tin. Turn out, scatter the pistachios over the top and serve.

# VANILLA PANNACOTTAS
# WITH BERRY COULIS

serves 6

This is my absolute favourite dessert. For me, if there is pannacotta on the menu, I find it hard to go past, even though there is not much about it that is good for you (except in this case the accompanying berry coulis and fresh berries are healthy). So, just enjoy it! I believe everyone should allow themselves an indulgence, but should just make sure it's not too often!

375 ml cream
185 ml milk
110 g (½ cup) sugar
1 vanilla pod, seeds scraped
3 teaspoons powdered gelatine (or
    2 sheets softened in cold water)
250 g raspberries
125 g blueberries

Put the cream, milk, sugar and vanilla pod and seeds in a saucepan over medium heat and stir until the sugar dissolves. Bring to a simmer and cook for 3 minutes, then remove from the heat and sprinkle over the powdered gelatine (or add the softened sheets). Whisk the gelatine in well. Strain the mixture into a large jug.

   Pour into six 125 ml moulds and leave to cool, then refrigerate for 3 hours, or until firm. Place half the raspberries and blueberries in a food processor and blend until smooth, forming the berry coulis.

   To serve, briefly dip the moulds into hot water and turn the pannacottas out onto plates. Serve with the berry coulis and remaining fresh berries.

BERRIES ALMOST SEEM LIKE CHEATING, AS THEY ARE SO GOOD FOR YOU AND EVERYONE LOVES THE FLAVOUR. THEY CONTAIN SOME OF THE HIGHEST LEVELS OF ANTIOXIDANTS AND ARE A FANTASTIC SOURCE OF FIBRE, VITAMIN C, FOLATE AND ZINC.

# FIGS WITH ROSEWATER
# AND GOAT'S CHEESE

serves 4

This may be the quickest dessert ever – it is rather like putting out a cheese plate, but the emphasis is on the fruit. Be warned, it is very more-ish.

2 tablespoons honey
1 tablespoon rosewater
8 figs, cut in half
freshly ground black pepper
40 g fresh goat's cheese, finely sliced
2 tablespoons pistachios, chopped

Preheat an oven grill to medium-high. Line a tray with baking paper.

Put the honey and rosewater in a small saucepan and heat gently until the honey is soft and runny.

Place the fig halves on the tray. Season with pepper and top with the slices of goat's cheese. Drizzle over the honey mixture. Grill for 5-6 minutes, or until the cheese is starting to melt. Sprinkle with the pistachios and serve.

ROSEWATER AND ROSE OIL ARE BOTH MADE FROM STEAM-DISTILLING ROSE PETALS. ROSEWATER HAS A SUBTLE YET DISTINCT FLORAL FLAVOUR, AND IS USED IN MANY MIDDLE EASTERN DESSERTS, WHETHER TURKISH OR IRANIAN. LOOK OUT FOR IT IN MIDDLE EASTERN STORES.

# CHERRY PUDDING

serves 10–12

Cherries are my favourite fruit, and I am lucky that my nan stews and preserves them for me so I can have them all year round. Of course, stewing fruit means it's not as good for you as fresh fruit without the sugar, but it's also making good use of something seasonal and not letting it spoil.

If you don't have stewed cherries, then cherries from a tin or jar will do. The recipe is based on a clafouti, but with extra fruit. It is all about the fruit, as there's not much sugar or flour in it.

800 g preserved pitted cherries
100 ml kirsch
6 eggs
1 teaspoon vanilla extract
3 tablespoons caster sugar
100 g (⅔ cup) plain flour
icing sugar to dust

Combine the cherries and kirsch in a bowl and leave to macerate for 30 minutes.

Preheat the oven to 220°C. Lightly butter a shallow round ceramic dish, about 25 cm in diameter.

Whisk the eggs, vanilla and sugar in a medium bowl until pale. Sift over the flour and gently fold in until just combined. Fold in the cherries and their juices. Pour the batter into the dish and bake for 40–45 minutes, or until golden and set (you can test it with a skewer). Dust with icing sugar and serve warm.

# MANGO AND BERRY SOUP

*serves 8*

This is a great summer dessert that is all fruit and no sugar. The mangoes and berries are pureed separately, then poured into bowls creating bright bursts of yellow and red – it presents beautifully at a dinner party. Lemon juice takes out some of the sweetness of the mango so it doesn't overpower the berries.

flesh of 3 mangoes
3 tablespoons lemon juice
450 g strawberries, hulled
125 g raspberries
¼ cup fresh spearmint (or mint) leaves
2 tablespoons pistachios, finely chopped

Put the mango and lemon juice in a food processor and blend until smooth. Pour the mixture into a jug. Rinse and dry the food processor, then blend the strawberries and raspberries together. Pour into another jug.

Select wide, shallow bowls to serve. Carefully pour the berry mixture into half of one bowl while at the same time pouring the mango mixture into the other half. The aim is to have two neat semicircles of yellow and red. Continue pouring the soup into the remaining bowls. Decorate with the spearmint leaves and chopped pistachios.

IF THERE IS A FRUIT THAT YOU LOVE THAT YOU KNOW YOU CAN ONLY GET FOR PART OF THE YEAR, SUCH AS MANGOES, THEN WHY NOT FREEZE THE FLESH SO YOU CAN HAVE A HEALTHY TREAT WHENEVER YOU WANT?

# NUTRITION TERMS
## EXPLAINED

Here's a list of common nutrition terms that are often used in relation to
a healthy lifestyle and balanced diet, and which are used in this book.

## KILOJOULES

Kilojoules, or calories, measure the energy-generating capacity of our food. Put simply, they show
us the amount of energy that foods provide us with – one calorie has the same value as 4.186
kilojoules. The energy content of foods depends on their ratio of carbohydrates, fats and proteins.
Carbohydrates have 16 kilojoules per gram, protein 17 kilojoules per gram, fat 37 kilojoules per
gram and alcohol 27 kilojoules per gram. Your body needs kilojoules for energy, but too many in
your diet and not enough movement to burn them off can lead to weight gain. Different body types
and lifestyles require different amounts of kilojoules per day; for example, I had to greatly reduce my
intake when I stopped training and no longer needed the same amount of energy. On average, an
adult female has a daily requirement of 9000 kilojoules and an adult male requires 11,000 kilojoules.

## CARBOHYDRATES

Carbohydrates are the body's preferred fuel source as they are quickly converted to glucose, the
body's main form of energy. (Other energy sources are fat and protein, but their conversion to
energy is less efficient.) The average adult should aim to consume 310 g of carbohydrates a day, or
in other words, sixty per cent of their energy intake should come from carbohydrates. When I am
training and competing, I have a very high amount of carbohydrates in my diet as I literally burn
them all off in the pool.

There are two main types of carbohydrates: 'simple' and 'complex', relating to what they are
made up of and how quickly they are absorbed and raise glucose levels in the blood. **Simple
carbohydrates** are sugars that are converted into energy quickly, but which also burn out just as
fast. Examples are sugar itself, as well as soft drinks, honey and some fruit. **Complex carbohydrates**
are starches that take longer to be digested and absorbed, and therefore give a slower release of
energy. Their slower digestion also means they are less likely to cause an overproduction of glucose,
which in turn is less likely to be stored as fat. Complex carbohydrates include grains and legumes,
rice, bread and potatoes. The best complex carbohydrates are those that are unrefined and contain
fibre, such as wholemeal bread or brown rice, as they are the slowest to be digested and absorbed,
so they provide sustained energy, and they also come with more nutrients.

## GLYCEMIC INDEX AND GLYCEMIC LOAD

The Glycemic Index is a ranking from zero to 100 (and sometimes above) given to foods to describe
how quickly the carbohydrate they contain is digested and absorbed into the blood. The scale
doesn't simply go from complex carbohydrates at the bottom through to simple carbohydrates at
the top, as some complex carbohydrates have a medium or high GI, such as white bread, white
rice and potatoes.

GI is an extremely important consideration for those with diabetes, as by eating low-GI foods, the body is able to control its blood glucose and insulin levels. **Low-GI foods** take longer to digest, which means they keep you feeling fuller for longer. Low-GI foods include wholegrain cereals, breads and pastas; beans and lentils; seeds and nuts; milk and yoghurt; vegetables such as broccoli, avocado and salad greens; and fruit such as apples, cherries, oranges, pears and plums.

**High-GI foods** include a lot of the white, refined stuff with 'empty' calories, such as white bread, white rice and breakfast cereals such as Rice Bubbles or cornflakes, and dates, watermelon and soft drinks.

However, to make matters slightly more confusing, it has been revealed that GI doesn't give the full picture – as it doesn't take into account the **quantity** of carbohydrate in foods, only the **quality** of the carbohydrate. Glycemic Load (GL) is based on GI as well as the amount of carbohydrate, and gives you a more accurate idea of how foods affect your body. It paints foods such as watermelon (with a high GI but a small amount of carbohydrate) in a much better light. How you combine food in meals is another factor that should be considered – as foods high in GI and GL combined with foods low in these things, such as high-fibre vegetables, also changes the effect on blood sugar.

Eating low GI and GL foods for slow energy release is really important for endurance sports. Considering the GI and GL value of foods can give an athlete a definite edge, as sometimes high GI and GL foods are needed for an energy burst, whereas in long hours of continuous exercise, low GI and GL foods are required.

## PROTEIN

Protein is the base of our muscles, skin and cells as well as our hormones, antibodies and enzymes. It is used to build and repair muscles, making it an especially important part of any athlete's diet. Protein can also provide the body with energy in the absence of adequate carbohydrates, but it does this slowly and in smaller amounts.

The protein we eat is digested to release amino acids, and while the body makes some of its own amino acids, there are others that must be supplied through food. Meat including fish is a well known source of protein (100 g of lean beef contains around 23 g of protein; 100 g of fish has 27 g), but other excellent sources include eggs and dairy products, beans, lentils, soy products, seeds and nuts. The recommended daily intake of protein is 46 g for women and 64 g for men, but this varies with an individual's weight. Like fibre, eating protein makes us feel full.

## FIBRE

Dietary fibre is extremely important for a healthy digestive system – even though it is actually indigestible. There are two types of fibre – insoluble and soluble. **Insoluble fibre** passes through the body relatively unchanged, adding bulk to the contents of our intestines and producing a laxative effect. **Soluble fibre** absorbs water and softens bowel movements, and is fermented by friendly bacteria in the large intestine to produce short-chain fatty acids that stabilise blood-glucose levels and can help to reduce low-density lipoprotein (LDL or 'bad') cholesterol. It is recommended that we eat 30 g of fibre a day to reduce such things as constipation and the risk of bowel cancer. Fibre is found in plant-based foods, which often have a combination of both soluble and insoluble fibre. Sources of insoluble fibre include wholegrain bread and cereals, bran, legumes and the skin of fruits and vegetables, while sources of soluble fibre include fruit and vegetables, oats, barley, legumes and seeds.

## SUGAR

Sugar is a simple carbohydrate that can be added to food or which naturally occurs in it. Some of the different types of sugar include table sugar (sucrose), sugar found in fruit (fructose), and sugar found in dairy foods (lactose). A small amount of sugar in the diet is okay – people generally assume that table sugar (sucrose) has a high GI, but in fact it has a moderate one of 65. But too much isn't good for you and, like all carbohydrates, if sugar isn't used as energy by the body, it is stored as fat. Food with naturally occurring sugar is always preferable to food with added sugar such as lollies and soft drinks (a 375 ml soft-drink can contains up to ten teaspoons of sugar!)

## SALT

Salt is composed of the minerals sodium and chloride, which naturally occur in animal products, plant foods and water and are essential nutrients in our diets. Sodium balances the amount of fluid in the body's tissues and blood, and helps with nerve and muscle function. However, excess sodium has adverse effects and today people commonly exceed the amount of sodium their bodies require, leading to high blood pressure, increasing the risk of strokes and heart disease, and also causing water retention. The Heart Foundation of Australia recommends a **maximum** sodium intake of 2300 mg (approximately 6 g or 1½ teaspoons of salt) a day for Australian's with normal blood pressure. Processed foods such as breakfast cereals, snack foods and tinned vegetables are generally very high in salt and contribute to seventy-five per cent of the salt intake in the average diet.

## FATS

Fats don't entirely deserve a bad wrap, as some are beneficial. Believe it or not, fat is actually classed as a nutrient and helps the body to absorb vitamins A, D, E and K. The good fats are monounsaturated and polyunsaturated fats. **Monounsaturated fats** are found in canola and olive oil, avocados and nuts. **Polyunsaturated fats** include Omega-3, which is found in oily fish such as salmon and sardines, as well as linseeds, walnuts, soy products and green leafy vegetables. It lowers LDL cholesterol and blood pressure and reduces the risk of heart disease. Omega-6 is another beneficial polyunsaturated fat found in nuts, seeds and plant-based oils such as soybean, corn and sunflower oil. However, it is over-consumed in the modern Western diet (i.e. cooking oil used in processed foods, and margarine) and has detrimental effects, even countering the benefits of Omega-3 and leading to conditions such as heart disease. So, most people today need to concentrate on their Omega-3 intake and reduce their Omega-6 intake.

Other fats to limit in your diet are saturated and trans fats. **Saturated fats** are found in animal products – fatty meats, processed meats and dairy products – and in some plant sources such as palm and coconut oil. **Trans fats** do occur naturally, but are also manufactured for use in margarine, shortening and factory-baked goods. Both of these fats behave similarly in our bodies and can increase the levels of LDL cholesterol and lead to heart disease.

## VITAMINS AND MINERALS

Vitamins are organic compounds that our bodies use for a variety of metabolic processes. Minerals are inorganic elements that are also just as necessary for health and wellbeing.

It's always best to get your vitamin and mineral needs from a varied diet, and supplements shouldn't be considered a substitute for balanced eating. Studies have shown that vitamins and minerals can be dangerous taken in large doses and 'out of context' – without the related compounds they occur with in foods. Here are just a few of the vitamins and minerals our bodies require and some of the foods they occur in:

**Calcium** is a vitamin that promotes healthy bones and teeth and works with vitamin K in clotting blood when we are wounded. Good sources of calcium include dairy products, broccoli, green beans, almonds, orange juice, salmon and sardines.

**Folate** is a B vitamin used for growing and repairing red blood cells. Good sources include asparagus, broccoli, spinach, legumes, mushrooms, oranges, bananas, strawberries and tuna.

**Vitamin A** promotes health in bones, teeth, skin and mucous membranes, and is an antioxidant. Great sources include many orange fruits and vegetables such as mangoes, apricots, carrots, pumpkin and sweet potatoes, along with spinach, broccoli and tuna.

**Vitamin C** is used in collagen production, boosts our immune system, and is an antioxidant. Oranges are a well-known source of vitamin C, but others are grapefruit, berries, kiwi fruit, capsicums, tomatoes, cabbage and broccoli.

**Vitamin D** is involved in calcium absorption as well as general bone and teeth health. The best source of vitamin D is sunlight, but it is also found in eggs, tuna and salmon.

**Vitamin E** is important for good circulation and healthy skin, and is an antioxidant. Good sources of vitamin E include oils, nuts, seeds, broccoli and mangoes.

**Iron** is a mineral used for carrying oxygen in the blood. Great sources are red meat, oysters, leafy greens, soy products, dried fruit and sesame and pumpkin seeds. However, iron from animal sources is better absorbed by our bodies. Vitamin C assists in iron absorption.

**Magnesium** is a mineral involved in the production of energy and the function of enzymes. Great sources of magnesium are nuts and seeds, grains, seafood, spinach, broccoli and bananas.

**Potassium** is a mineral that helps in the functioning of nerves and muscles and in controlling blood pressure. Good sources are meat, milk, avocados, spinach, tomatoes, pumpkin, mushrooms and bananas.

**Zinc** is a mineral that supports the immune system, helps with wound healing and is an antioxidant. It is found in meat, fish, oysters, dairy products, wheatgerm and legumes.

## ANTIOXIDANTS

Antioxidants are compounds found in certain foods that help to fight off the damaging effects of chemicals called free radicals. Free radicals come about when oxidation occurs in the body, and can be accelerated by environmental factors such as pollution, smoking, stress and overexposure to sunlight. The body can't cope with an overload of free radicals, and they can eventually lead to serious conditions such as heart disease and cancer, which is why antioxidant-rich food should feature in our diets. Antioxidants neutralise cell damage and keep the body healthy. Just some of the great antioxidants include vitamins C and E and beta-carotene, which is a precursor to vitamin A and found in the same foods; flavonoids (found in green tea, red wine, citrus fruit and pomegranates); and lycopene (found in tomatoes and pink grapefruit).

# INDEX ~

# ACKNOWLEDGEMENTS

I'd like to thank all my family and friends who have encouraged me to write this book. To my family — you have been such a source of inspiration, knowledge and support. And to my friends who share the dinner table with me — I appreciate your company always (especially when you offer to clean up! For this I have an extra-big thanks for Lis.).

In particular I'd like to thank my grandmothers Nanny Hathaway and Nanny Thorpe – they taught me to make my first cakes and also that leftovers are not just frugal, but delicious. (Bubble and squeak, anyone?)

I would also like to thank my mum for allowing me to cook the family meal on Sundays from when I was ten years old, and persisting through a couple of disasters.

Extra thanks are due to the many chefs who have allowed me to spend time in their kitchens over the years, learning some great lessons that have helped shape me into the cook I am.

Special thanks to the talented crew who breathed life into such a fantastic-looking book.

To the Vales, for allowing me to use the boathouse and providing the best location for so many barbecues – thank you.

And in no particular order, thanks to Samantha Jennings, Patrick Darwen, Naomi Kenny, Christian Miranda, Ryan Beaven, Carly Rogerson, Timothy Addison, Joanne, Leonard, Simone Kessel, Greggor Jordan and Jack Jordan for helping out and giving up some of their weekend to be part of this book.

This edition published in 2016

Hardie Grant Books (Australia)
Ground Floor, Building 1
658 Church Street
Richmond, Victoria 3121
www.hardiegrant.com.au

Hardie Grant Books (UK)
5th & 6th Floors
52-54 Southwark Street
London SE1 1UN
www.hardiegrant.co.uk

A Cataloguing-in-Publication entry is available from the catalogue of the National Library of Australia at www.nla.gov.au
Eat Well Now
ISBN 978 17437 91547

Publisher: Pam Brewster
Editor: Rachel Pitts
Cover and text design: Andy Warren
Page layout and typesetting: Andy Warren
Studio photography: Gorta Yuuki
Studio stylist: Simon Bajada
Studio food preparation: Toula Ploumidis
Location photography: William Meppem
Location stylist: Emma Knowles
Location food preparation: Ian Thorpe

The publishers would like to thank the following for supplying props: The Works Bed Bath and Table, Mud, Bison, Angelucci, Great Dane Furniture.

Colour reproduction by Splitting Image Colour Studio
Printed in China by 1010 Printing International Limited